Researching Early Childhood Education: European Perspectives

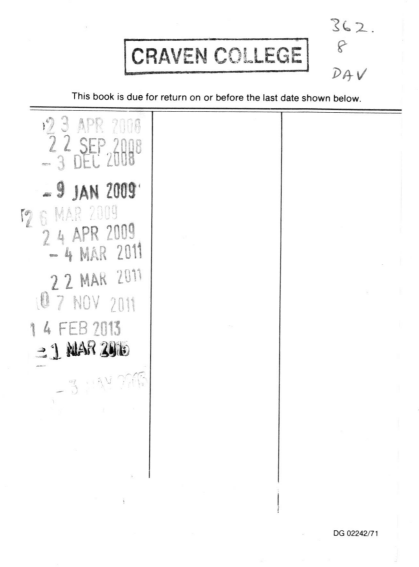

Researching Early Childhood Education: European Perspectives

edited by

Tricia David

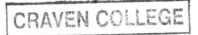

P·C·P

Paul Chapman
Publishing Ltd

Paul Chapman Publishing Ltd
A SAGE Publications Company
6 Bonhill Street
London EC2A 4PU

SAGE Publications Inc.
2455 Teller Road
Thousand Oaks, California 91320

SAGE Publications India Pvt Ltd
32, M-Block Market
Greater Kailash-I
New Delhi 110 048

British Cataloguing in Publication Data

Researching early childhood education: European perspectives
1. Early childhood education – Research – Europe
I. David, Tricia, 1942–
372.2'1'072'04

ISBN 1 85396 419 0
ISBN 1 85396 356 9 (pbk)

Library of Congress catalog card number

Typeset by Anneset, Weston-super-Mare, Somerset
Printed and bound in Great Britain by Athenaeum Press, Gateshead
ABCDEF 321098

Contents

The authors: biographical details

Teresa Aguado is Associate Professor of Research Methods in the Education Department at UNED (the Open University of Spain). Her doctoral thesis presented an analysis and evaluation of experimental preschool programmes developed during the national reforms in Spain. She is the author of a number of articles and books about early and preschool education and she has collaborated with the Ministry of Education on several training courses for teachers in this field.

Associate Professor Stig Broström was born in Denmark in 1945 and educated as a kindergarten teacher. He has been a tutor at a college for teacher education and since 1994 at the Royal Danish School of Educational Studies. His main areas of research are in the field of day-care centres and transition to school.

Tricia David is a Professor of Education at Canterbury Christ Church College, where she directs the Centre for International Studies in Early Childhood. She is a past President of OMEP UK (OMEP is the World Organisation for Early Childhood Education) and she is currently a member of BERA (British Educational Research Association) Council and the editor of the *International Journal of Early Childhood*. Tricia and her colleagues are about to embark on a two-year, comparative research and development project on early literacy, funded by the Esmée Fairbairn Foundation.

Nóirín Hayes is Head of the School of Social Sciences at the Dublin Institute of Technology. Her particular area of interest is early child development and education. She is author of the book *Early Childhood: An Introductory Text* (1993). She is currently directing the Irish element of the IEA Pre-Primary Project and is co-author of *A Window on Early Education in Ireland* (1997), the first national report of this project. In addition she is directing a European Union project on Childcare Training in Ireland.

Rosario Jiminez-Frias is an Associate Professor at the Department of Research Methods in Education at UNED, Spain. She has written several books and articles on early childhood education and is a contributor to a number of training courses promoted by the Ministry of Education, for this field. Her specialism is the elaboration of didactical discourses and the implementation of courses at national level.

Malgorzata Karwowska-Struczyk PhD has been involved in early childhood education for 20 years, as a psychologist working with abandoned children, as a researcher in the field of child development and education, and as a teacher educator at Warsaw University Department of Early Childhood. She has written over 100 articles and contributions to books, some translated into English. Malgorzata has co-operated with the Van Leer Foundation and for the last six years she has been the Polish co-ordinator for the international High/Scope-IEA comparative research *Quality of Life* study. She is a member of the World Association for Case Method Research and Application (WACRA) and of OMEP (World Organisation for Early Childhood Education).

Alkistis Kondoyianni, author, kindergarten teacher and instructor of Drama in Education, has taught Drama at Athens University Department of Early Childhood Education (1989–1994) and at the Department of Theatre Studies (1994–1997). She is now working for the Ministry of Education as an adviser for Drama in Education. Her PhD explored the social competence of children with learning disabilities through drama education. She is the author of 48 educational books for children and teachers. Alkistis has been the Chairperson of OMEP Greece since 1992.

Ulla Lind, Master of Arts in Art Education, is a doctoral student at the Stockholm Institute of Education Department of Child Pedagogy and Youth Studies. She is a lecturer and researcher in applied semiotics, visual-aesthetic communication and learning and socialisation processes. Her work also covers the discourses interacting in art education and pedagogy among children and youth.

Dr Helen Penn is Senior Research Fellow at the Social Science Research Unit, Institute of Education, London University. She has published many reports and books on early years. Her most recent book is *Comparing Nurseries* (Paul Chapman, 1997). She has recently completed a review of Early Childhood Services in Developing and

Transitional Countries for the Department of International Development, and works with a variety of organisations and government research departments in a wide range of countries.

Eric Plaisance is Professor in the Department of Science of Education at the Université René Descartes. He directs the Sociologie de l'Education Research Unit, associated with the Centre National de la Recherche Scientifique (CNRS). Eric is also President of the Conseil Scientifique of the Faculté des Sciences Humaines et Sociales-Sorbonne. His doctoral thesis is a systematic analysis of French nursery schools after the Second World War. This was published under the title *L'enfant, la maternelle et la societé*. His most recent publications are: *Les sciences de l'éducation* and *Pauline Kergomard et l'école maternelle; Preschool education today* (for a special edition of the *Revue Française de Pédagogie*, with Sylvie Rayna) and a comparative study of education for disabled children: *L'exclusion, l'état des savoirs*.

Sylvie Rayna is 'maître de conferences' in psychology of education at the Institut National de Recherche Pédagogique, where she has carried out studies in early childhood and psychology since the early 1970s. She has been involved in several action-research projects in daycare centres through CRESAS (Centre de Recherches sur l'Education Specialisée et l'Adaptation Scolaire) whose research agenda is the prevention of school failure, exploring the constructive role of social action and peer interaction. Sylvie is currently involved in studies about early childhood education policy and the 'new professionals' – early childhood co-ordinators. She has co-authored several books in French and English, including *Pretend Play among Three-Year-Olds* (with Ballion, Bréauté and Stambak, published by Lawrence Erlbaum Associates).

Karin Vilien was born in Denmark in 1945. She was educated as a kindergarten teacher and school teacher and she holds an MA in Education from the University of Copenhagen. She worked as a college tutor of advanced studies for kindergarten teachers and at the Royal School of Educational Studies. She is now working as private consultant in development work in kindergartens and primary schools. Karin was also a contributor to the collection of papers which preceded this text, *Educating our Youngest Children: European Perspectives* (Paul Chapman, 1993).

Acknowledgements

This book would not have been written if it were not for the international networks of colleagues who have supported all of us, the contributors to this text. In particular, I as editor must thank friends in OMEP (L'Organisation Mondiale pour l'Education Préscolaire); EECERA (European Early Childhood Education Research Association) and the Warwick University Early Years Conference for their influence in bringing together so many practitioners, researchers, administrators and others whose working lives are devoted to young children and their families. Where authors have received special financial support, they have acknowledged this in their chapters and this support is gratefully acknowledged here also.

Every publication requires considerable effort behind the scenes, so many thanks are also due to Marianne Lagrange, Joyce Lynch and the former PCP team, together with their new Sage colleagues, for their patience, effort and sound advice, and to Louise Duff in particular at Canterbury Christ Church College for her unstinting support.

Each contributor has her own 'family and friends' list of acknowledgements and dedications. Mine is, as ever: Roy, Sacha and Ceris, now plus Dave and Colin, and the book is dedicated to my amazing and adorable, very small grandchildren, Coralie and Eliot.

Tricia David
Canterbury Christ Church College
June 1998

1

Introduction: Researching Early Childhood Education in Europe

Tricia David

In 1993, a group of early childhood educators from eight Western European countries contributed to a book in which we tried to describe our respective histories and systems for educating children in the years before the primary school stage (David, 1993). This second book is a natural step in that attempt to make sense of our own and other countries' ideas about and plans for the youngest children in our community. In this publication some of the authors are the same as in the last, some are not. Similarly, the countries included in some cases overlap with the last book and others are 'new'. In particular, this book includes one Eastern European country, to help us begin a wider exploration of our commonalities and our differences.

No book covering only eight states could claim comprehensively to cover European early childhood education research, but in that this one contains reports from countries which are geographically in the north, south, east and west of the land mass, some which are relatively small or have small populations and others which are large and densely populated, perhaps it will serve as a basis for further exploration. The countries included are: Denmark, France, Greece, Ireland, Poland, Spain, Sweden and the UK.

Additionally, the second chapter, by Helen Penn, who has had the opportunity to research and work with early years practitioners within both Europe and other continents, raises questions about the feasibility of comparative research, its problems and pitfalls, and suggests a way forward. These are important questions, not only because we are forced to go back to our assumptions and our own histories to heighten our awareness of the research approaches which may be possible, but also because language barriers and interpretations sometimes hide misunderstandings. Here, researchers are writing about the situations in their own countries, but we must still be vigilant of misinterpretations and of believing research in our own country has nothing to learn from other research communities and other cultures.

Malgorzata Karwowska-Struczyk recounts a host of developments in Poland, within the context of a country developing democracy and getting to grips with the capitalist system. Alkistis Kondoyianni provides a wealth of references to early years education research, reported in English, undertaken in Greece, pointing out that this collection is purely a starting point and thus indicating the healthy research climate despite issues of funding and the lack of a central 'bank' of research work. In their survey of the situation in Spain, Teresa Aguado and Rosario Jiminez Frias highlight the relatively recent development of early childhood research and the current gap between practitioners and researchers, so prevalent in most European countries. They also provide a 'wish list' for the future. The account of the present state of French early education research by Sylvia Rayna and Eric Plaisance discusses authoritatively the main foci of researchers and the difficulties raised by contract research, since much work there is carried out by specialist units for which early childhood is only a small part of their potential brief. From Ireland, Nóirín Hayes strikingly sets early years research developments in context. Those of us in the UK find we echo many of the issues relating to early formalisation discussed by Irish researchers and practitioners. Ulla Lind's chapter describes an advanced and exciting research culture in Sweden, she may well stimulate new, postmodern and feminist developments in the countries where such approaches have been neglected.

Although the Organisation for Economic Co-operation and Development (OECD) comprises a wider membership than European states (the members of the OECD are: Australia, Austria, Belgium, Canada, Denmark, Finland, France, Germany, Greece, Iceland, Ireland, Italy, Japan, Luxembourg, Mexico, the Netherlands, New Zealand, Norway, Portugal, Spain, Sweden, Switzerland, Turkey, the United Kingdom and the United States of America), a recent OECD report (OECD 1995) provides some relevant and useful internationally-based discussion of a number of the issues which confront those working in the early years education research field. For example, in a chapter considering 'What is educational research?', the OECD Secretary-General (aided by the work of Professor Maurice Kogan and Albert Tuijnman) argues that there is no international agreement about the precise meaning of the term 'educational research and development' and the report proposes the following definition

> Educational R & D is systematic, original investigation or inquiry and
> associated development activities concerning the social, cultural, eco-

nomic and political contexts within which education systems operate and learning takes place; the purposes of education; the processes of teaching, learning and personal development of children, youth and adults; the work of educators; the resources and organisational arrangements to support educational work; the policies and strategies to achieve educational objectives; and the social, cultural, political and economic outcomes of education.

(OECD 1995, p. 37).

As the report points out, there can be a danger in making the definition of 'educational research' too wide, or too narrow but, as they argue, much research that is useful to the field of education actually goes on in departments in institutions of higher education focusing on other disciplines, such as sociology, psychology or economics and that to make the definition allow for, say, a narrow research base in classrooms, would exclude much that is important to our understanding of learners and their lives.

A further point made by this OECD report relevant to our early years research overview is the relative youth of educational research. It is argued that in fact the first tradition or paradigm to emerge in educational research was really the approach associated with hermeneutics and critical philosophy, seeking to 'understand' 'What should be in education?' (OECD 1995, p. 33) and that the positivist paradigm, with its roots in natural sciences, seeking explanations, emerged towards the end of the nineteenth century. Certainly, the field of early childhood education research seems to have been dominated by natural science assumptions and methods during this century, but it may be that this, more than educational research relating to older learners, has been greatly influenced by developmental psychology. During the last twenty years both educational research and developmental psychology have been wrestling with the the challenges thrown up by different approaches and models or paradigms of 'how the world works' and therefore how to conduct research. A related issue which must be addressed by the educational research field as a whole, including those in early years research settings, is the questioning of 'certainty'. For example, in the USA the Committee on the Federal Role of Education Research (1992) rejected a linear model based on the expectation that research could show causes, lead to 'improvements' and so solve problems quite simply. However, the Committee came to the conclusion that it was still important to invest substantial sums in educational research, particularly in the founding of 'learning communities . . . partnerships among researchers, practitioners and policy-makers, in which each becomes involved in disciplined inquiry and each contributes to the learning of the others' (US National Academy of Sciences 1992, p. 17). The OECD report concludes that educational research has much to offer the field, the weakness seems to be that it has not been fully exploited. Perhaps some of the problems lie in the modes and costs of dissemination – the chapter by Stig Broström and Karin Vilien in this book provides an example of how the Danish preschool teachers' union plays a very active role in encouraging and disseminating research findings. While the OECD report seems to favour greater sharing of knowledge among researchers, practitioners and policy-makers, and this is to be welcomed, there is also a need to ask to what extent all the parties involved require the same type of information about particular issues or different aspects of findings concerning the issues. Parents and carers too should be involved and they might need yet another form and style of dissemination.

Other factors which impact on educational research include the economy and trends can be detected in both the funding of and national/governmental interest in research concerning learning in very young children which are due to fluctuations in the economy. Although individual authors have commented where this is relevant in their contributions, a fuller discussion of this issue, among others, relating to researching early childhood education, although focusing mainly on the UK, can be found in Aubrey, David and Thompson (forthcoming).

The themes which seem to recur through the different chapters in this early years publication tend to be those associated with the difficulties of conducting early childhood education research, usually through funding problems rather than through issues related to access or reluctance on the part of practitioners. In fact practitioner research too is encouraged more or less universally. Research programmes tend to be dictated by governments – both central and local – or by powerful research councils. While individual researchers based in universities and schools can choose their own foci for projects if they are self-funded, they must satisfy funding bodies (occasionally their employing institution) if they wish to gain the necessary monies to carry out the work. During times when government policies may run counter to researchers' better judgements (based on earlier research which has gone unheeded), it may be necessary to adopt what I like to call the *Mozart-Titian technique*. This means one proposes research which will be of interest to sponsors and carries it out at the same time as using the opportunity to gather information for work which will be a true expression of one's own interests. If this approach was good enough for Mozart and Titian, who not only gave us a heritage of masterpieces in music and art but also explored the 'frontiers' of their disciplines, then it's good enough for me anyway.

If we wish to generate debate about what early childhood is, what it means to be a young child in a particular society and what educational services should be provided as a result, we, the researchers, need to make our debate more accessible to a wider audience, we need to befriend the press, parents and politicians alike. Further, we need to encourage our teacher and educator colleagues to become involved in research projects, to share in the excitement of exploring, thinking, writing – activities which, certainly in Britain, are rarely recognised as real work requiring sufficient time to carry out properly.

Although early childhood education research forms only a fraction of the remit in the OECD (1995) report, some very useful overviews of educational research are included from Australia, Austria, Germany, the Netherlands, Portugal, Sweden, Switzerland and the United States. That a number of other countries are not included in this publication does not signify a lack of interest in them on our part as collaborating authors – quite the contrary. Each time we, as early years educators and researchers, meet at international conferences there is much to discuss and much to learn from colleagues representing countries throughout the world. As communications and travel have improved, so too has our ability to support each other and to share ideas. Further, when a group of early years researchers meet together, they usually find they have far more in common than differences between them. The boundaries which have separated us are growing less and less obvious. While in some senses we are witnessing the homogenisation of Europe, there are other aspects of life in which regional concerns dominate. Although this book seeks to share research perspectives in early childhood education, it must be remembered that children's lives are far wider than this limited field, yet what is provided for them as education will impinge on their lives and those of their family members now and cast shadows into the future. Countries which can see the value in high quality research and the discussions it can generate among its people seem likely to have a clear and open view of their vision for their country's development and how it needs to be owned by the members of its society.

References

Aubrey, C., David, T. and Thompson, L. (forthcoming) *Researching Early Childhood Education: Methodological and Ethical Issues.* London: Falmer Press.

David, T. (ed.) (1993) *Educating our Youngest Children: European Perspectives*. London: Paul Chapman.

OECD (1995) *Educational Research and Development: Trends, Issues and Challenges*. Paris: Organisation for Economic Co-operation and Development.

US National Academy of Science (1992) *Research and Education Reform*. Washington, DC: National Academy Press.

2

Comparative Research: a Way Forward?

Helen Penn

Introduction: who or what is a child?

Over the last ten years I have been fortunate enough to spend time working in a variety of countries outside my own, in Europe and in the Majority World.[1] Working in this way has been an eye-opening and enriching experience, and it becomes impossible to view the world through one set of standards. On the contrary, I am aware of a continuum of perspectives on what childhood is, how children should be brought up, and what kind of collective arrangements it is possible to make on their behalf.

As Jahoda and Lewis (1988) demonstrate in their review of anthropological research on childhood, children experience daily life in very different ways, differences which go far beyond daily income and the immediate emotional climate created by the child's carers. To understand childhood requires an understanding of the cultural codes in the society or communities in which the child is located. I have argued in a discussion paper for UNICEF (Penn, 1997c) that childhood is constructed on the basis of many assumptions, and children are positioned in many different ways, for example:

- as an individual or as part of a group

- as part of a nuclear family or as part of a complex kinship system

- as mainly in the company of peers or part of mixed age/intergenerational communities

[1] I follow recent usage in adopting the term 'Majority World' to describe what was previously called the 'Third World' or 'Developing World', and 'Minority World' to describe the industrialized countries of the North, in order to emphasise their position in relation to one another.

- as settled or nomadic
- as settled or migrant
- as living in a safe and protected environment or living in situations where exposure to physical risk and hardship is a necessary and valued experience
- as living in a politically stable or a war-torn environment
- as monolingual or multilingual
- as self-expressive or conformist and self-monitoring
- as aggressive or as equable and tender
- as having no obligations or responsibilities in the household or expected to contribute
- being cared for or caring for others
- learning through formalised institutional settings or learning through apprenticeship and work
- as owning possessions and property or sharing and communal use
- as being secular, religion as peripheral, or being deeply spiritual and naturalistic
- as cognitive or as aesthetic and musical
- as overtly genderless or as fundamentally gendered.

A typical configuration of a child in the Minority World child development literature, the child who is the focus of 'child-centred' early childhood development programmes, would revolve around the characteristics given first in the alternatives listed above, that is as an individual, separate from others, who is part of a nuclear family, cared for mainly by her mother, who lives in a permanent residence in a country which is not at war, is typically monolingual, who mixes mainly with same-age peers of the same social group, who could be expected to demonstrate instances of temper, aggression or social withdrawal, who is treated as childlike rather than adult-like, whose self-expressiveness is encouraged, who has few if any responsibilities, who is cared for rather than exercising care for others, who is encouraged to spend her time inventing her own games rather than contribute to any economic activity, who owns possessions and is reluctant to share them, who is not spiritual, who is to be guarded against physical risk, and who has little or no knowledge of the physical terrain in which she lives, has no survival skills, whose cognitive development takes priority over training in musical or artistic traditions or physical skills, and who at least overtly is treated as genderless.

This kind of 'normal' child would be unrecognisable, or regarded as severely dysfunctional, in many Majority World communities. Nelson Mandela, for example, recalls in his autobiography that he never recalls being alone at any time, day or night, until he was seven. His entire early childhood was spent in a mixed age group of children in his immediate kinship group, and with a variety of adults who shared responsibility for him – although his mother was foremost amongst them. Like the other children he was required to undertake certain communal responsibilities from the earliest possible age, such as herding animals, although he was also allowed to play freely once his duties were done, to run, to swim, to wrestle and engage in physical rough and tumble. He was always required to show respect and dutifulness to those adults with whom he shared his life – no disrespect to adults was possible. As a young child, no temper tantrums, no vigorous expression of individual wants were permitted. Few children had any possessions, and those they had were mainly shared. There was no consumerism to tempt them and enlarge their wants; their lives were characterised by a degree of frugality we can no longer imagine. This upbringing was very different from the one we now try to offer children in the UK, but it does not necessarily imply any kind of cognitive, social, moral or physical inferiority of development.

The status of child development as a basis for practice

Although there is now a considerable wealth of criticism of traditional child development, surprisingly little of it is taught to or known about by practitioners. The idea of developmentally appropriate practice (Bredekamp, 1987), 'ages and stages' of growth and development through which all young children pass, has been widely adopted in the Majority as well as the Minority World, and vocational training for work with children relies heavily upon it. Yet there has been a continual undercurrent of protest. Ogbu (1981) illustrates the indignation expressed by minority ethnic groups in the USA about the narrowness and the implicit political manipulation of conventional approaches to child development in the Head Start programme in the USA (often cited as an example of the importance of quality early learning).

This deficit perspective is nowhere more fully articulated than in the various preschool programs for 'disadvantaged children' begun in the 1960s. These programs are based on assumptions that an early acquisition of competencies is critical for later functioning in school and society, and that children's experiences with certain types of 'curriculum' during the preschool years promote optimal development, and that it is possible to correct developmental deficits through intervention programs for preschoolers and/or preventative programs directed at parents. The emphasis of a particular program tells us what instrumental competencies are presumed 'missing' in minority child rearing and development. For example, we know what competencies are thought to be missing when programs are designed to increase parents' knowledge of the core of effective child rearing through lectures, counselling, group discussion and the like; when programs attempt to train mothers in techniques of cognitive stimulation and social training by showing them how and how much to talk to and play with their children; or when programs aim to develop children's cognitive, social-emotional, pre-academic skills, or a combination of these competencies.

(Ogbu, 1981, pp. 413–29)

As Ogbu argues, the programs are designed to give ethnic minority children in America 'self-esteem' and other competencies in order to cope with living in one of the most unequal societies in the world – where black males have lower life expectancy than males in Bangladesh, the world's poorest country (de Vylder, 1996). Yet poor parenting rather than inequality is thought to be the source of the problem, or at least improving parenting along middle class lines is regarded as one of its remedies.

Moderate critics like Bronfenbrenner (1979) still hold to universalistic notions of child development, but stress the importance of seeing children in their social context (although remaining very vague as to what constitutes the social). More radical theorists argue that the conventional child development precepts are simply inapplicable outside the narrow contexts in which they were derived, and that the empirical methods devised for investigating them do not work in other places. Shweder (1990) in a much quoted article argues that learning can only be viewed as 'situated cognition'; that is, the notion that *all* learning is a creation of meaning in a highly specific context, and universal processes cannot per se exist. He and some others now argue that the term *cultural psychology* should be adopted rather than developmental psychology. Cole (1996), another leading theorist in the field, sees *cultural psychology* as domain specific, an attempt to derive principles from activities located at the level of everyday practice, and to use those practices as grounding for theoretical claims. There is a considerable overlap with anthropology, but cultural psychology maintains its interest in change and development within individuals, as well as with the characteristics of groups and communities.

Rogoff and Chavajay (1995) attempt to summarise recent work in the field of cultural psychology and on culture and cognition. They show how early cross-cultural work on cognition, where culture was viewed as an independent variable, has been superseded by a position where 'cognition involves communication in the context of institutional and cultural practices . . . and how communities and individuals manage diverse practices across overlapping and separate institutions and communities' (Rogoff and Chavajay, 1995, p. 873).

Recent books and papers by Stainton Rogers and Stainton Rogers (1992) and by Lubeck (1996) offer a critique of practice from a different, postmodern point of view, putting forward the argument that in most scientific fields of enquiry relativism or multiple viewpoints are emerging, and psychology cannot continue with empirical and universalistic approaches that have been discredited elsewhere. Whether from a cultural psychology or postmodernist point of view, there is now widespread recognition that the precepts of child development have been derived mainly from the experiences of Anglo-American middle class children. The difference is that, whilst cultural psychology still believes in the possibility of describing an overall picture of humanity, but one in which the full extent of human diversity is recognised and given its due, the postmodernists argue there can never be a whole picture, only alternative 'stories', that is, different and competing accounts, each according to who is telling the tale.

Yet as I argued at the beginning of this section, despite these new and radical perspectives within the discipline of child development, entrenched notions of a universalistic child development as a 'scientific' basis to practice still remain. A recent World Bank document claims for example that:

> A quarter of a century of US preschool research has identified several features that successful centerbased programmes share ... both research and experience have taught us that many principles of early education are universal ... to develop children's mental skills adults frequently read to them and engage them in conversation.
>
> (Young, 1996, p. 4)

This prescriptive document, of which I have included only the briefest extract, draws exclusively on American research for its assumptions of universality – for example, it assumes the availability of toys for children and reading materials. This is unlikely in many communities where possessions are few; where there may be powerful oral traditions, but no written ones; and where children would simply not be treated as conversational fellows.

Other perspectives on children and childhood

There have also been a number of recent studies offering a comparison at the level of services and practice in early childhood institutions (Lamb *et al.*, 1992; Cochran, 1993; Lewis, 1995; Tobin, Wu and Davidson, 1989) These too have to an extent been inspired by a realisation of the limitations of an Anglo-American perspective, and the desire to show how alternatives work. Lamb concludes that unequivocally the nature of the society, and in particular the position accorded to women, influences the kinds of arrangements which are made for children.

There is also a growing field of sociology and history of childhood, which considers children as a class or group of people characterised by powerlessness and which attempts to trace how they are acted upon by others (James and Prout, 1990). The Norwegian-based journal *Childhood* offers a forum for discussion on interpretations of childhood and within the UK, the Economic and Social Research Council (ESRC) has commissioned a programme of work on childhood.

The view of children as an oppressed group has given rise to the movement concerning children's rights, crystallised in the Human Rights declaration of the rights of the child, although as some commentators have pointed out, even to categorise children's rights as 'universal' constitutes a globalisation of childhood which is problematic (Boyden, 1990).

Cultural psychology then converges with anthropology, sociology, social policy and history in attempting to understand childhood, to see children in their time and space, and explain and modify the arrangements which are made for them (Elder, Model and Parke, 1993).

Research methodologies

As well as the debates about theoretical perspectives recounted above, there is also a vigorous debate about research methodologies, and about the place of empirical and quantitative and qualitative research methods. The methods are 'tools' for enquiry, but some theoretical perspectives require that only certain tools be used (Reinharz, 1992;

Hammersley, 1993; Stainton Rogers and Stainton Rogers, 1992). The methodologies researchers choose hinge on discussions of reality and meaning to diverse audiences, academic and non-academic. Deciding what is important and worth examining, choosing a particular methodology to examine it, recording, talking and writing about the data collected, are all contentious. There is no unambiguous foolproof way of doing research, of following the thread of an idea through the maze of practice and then explaining it to others. Knowing about and being skilled in a range of techniques, qualitative as well as quantitative, selecting with care those techniques that might be most appropriate for the questions you are asking – or being asked of you - understanding the strengths of those methods as well as their pitfalls, are necessary but not sufficient. In the last resort as a researcher one is judged not by the elegance nor immaculateness of the methodology, nor by the coherence and subtlety of the analysis, but by the relevance of the findings to one's theoretical stance, and to one's chosen audience,

Relevance to practice for me is a key issue. All research in social sciences is necessarily formed by social and political assumptions, of which one is often unaware. A frequent point of view expressed by researchers (Tizard, 1990; Schaffer, 1990) is that although they too may be wittingly or unwittingly influenced by current trends and events, they have a repertoire of techniques which enables them to stand back and take a more dispassionate view of the issues under question. This is a view of the researcher as subcontractor, undertaking an excavation of a particular piece of knowledge, or replumbing of information, at the behest of policy-makers or funders; research as a jobbing trade. But this perspective minimises the commitment of the researcher and places research as a job on the sidelines of policy, with all the concomitant problems of 'dissemination'.

Goldberger and Veroff (1995) in their overview of cultural psychology writings insist on the interdependence and interactive effects of different cultural traditions, particularly where, as in ethnically diverse societies, they operate side by side. They argue that researchers have what amounts to a duty as enablers of dialogue in and across the various communities in which they work – yet another slant on how and why research might be conducted.

Doing comparative research

Because I have travelled a great deal, I have become interested in comparative research methods, but they present very particular problems.

On one level, comparative research involves extracting and comparing existing research findings across countries; for example, comparing educational or financial statistics, or epidemiological surveys, or as in this book, comparing research strategies in different countries. The usual caveat about comparative research is that it is necessary to be acutely aware of the parameters under which the data was collected, the populations it describes and so on. Comparative research cannot be a straightforward matching of experiences, just as translation from one language to another is not a straightforward exchange of words.

But if we take on board the critique of cultural psychologists in looking at children and childrearing practices, which is that childhood is an ambiguous and disputed area where meanings are continually created and recreated, comparative research is very challenging. (A postmodernist might argue, more radically, that systematic comparative research is impossible, and that all that is possible is to listen to the separate voices and try to hear their stories.) It becomes important to use methodologies of investigation which do not obscure diversities of experience, but seek instead to highlight them. Setting aside the big questions about why the research is being conducted in the first place, and what assumptions it draws on, the specific methodological approach 'how can I get at the information I need in order to explore the boundaries and depths of the issue I am investigating?' is still more pertinent and subtle. It means in the first instance using techniques which are open-ended and alert to a range of practices; secondly developing methods which offer a contextual approach to understanding the practices under investigation; thirdly it implies some degree of reflexivity or self-awareness on the part of the investigator(s) about how they in turn might be perceived by those they are investigating; and fourthly it requires reciprocity and an attempt to use the information given for the benefit of those who contributed to it.

There are a number of classic comparative studies which illustrate how this might be done. One frequently cited piece of work is that of Shirley Brice Heath (1983) who used participant observer methods over a period of several years to try to understand and describe the separate idioms and language of black and white children in a small American town. She joined in family meals, she took children on outings, she attended church and community events, and noted any phrasings she thought were of interest, and the situation in which they occurred. She then tried to work with local schools to incorporate her findings, and persuaded them to deal sensitively and sympathetically with the social and linguistic traditions to which she had drawn attention.

Another revealing – and extremely generously funded – project by Tobin, Wu and Davidson (1989) compared practices in nurseries in China, Japan and the USA. They made extensive use of video-recordings in the nurseries, and then showed the videotapes to each of the other practitioner groups, inviting the Americans to comment on the Japanese, the Japanese on the Chinese and so on.

Both these projects took dissemination seriously, that is, offering to give back and extend the understandings and meanings they investigated to those who created them for comment and discussion and as a basis for analysing practices. Heath and Tobin took issues of practitioner relevance as central to their work. They viewed knowledge not as a nugget of truth to be displayed in the showcase of an academic journal, but as a step in the development of practice working with young children.

Comparative Research in Europe

I have been involved in a number of European-wide and comparative projects on early childhood. I will describe them here to illustrate the general points I have been making about the importance of using research methodologies which are alert to diversity, and which can be used as part of a process of developing practice.

First of all I have been involved in some of the work of the European Commission Childcare Network. Networks have been a standard way of working in the EU. Typically each country is asked to nominate a representative or 'expert' and the experts then work together on issues of current interest. The Childcare Network was set up to look at childcare and other measures to reconcile work and family life. It attempted to compare and co-ordinate the views and understandings of practitioners/researchers from each of the member states through a series of seminars and working parties. As is fairly well known, the systems in each European country differ considerably – a universalist-welfare-based system in Scandinavia; an education-based system in Spain and Italy; a split between under-threes in welfare and over-threes in education in France and Belgium; and hybrid and somewhat fragmented arrangements with overlapping welfare and education systems in the UK, Ireland, the Netherlands, Portugal and Greece. Within this context of diverse experiences and systems of early years care and education, there have been systematic attempts to compare the extent and content of provision, in a series of publications issued by the Network (ECN, 1996b). In particular I have been involved in the preparation of two discussion documents *Quality in Services to Young Children* (Balaguer, Mestres and Penn, 1992) and *Quality Targets in Services for Young Children* (European Childcare Network, 1996b) which were written over a period of seven years. I worked on the first drafts of these documents with colleagues from Spain, and they were then discussed at seminars for a wider group of researchers and practitioners, in the individual countries and then at a European seminar. They were redrafted as a result of the discussions, and then subjected to comment by the Network experts. These discussion documents represent negotiated views about practice and the way to develop it; but as well as offering a benchmark, they offer a methodology of working. They provide a perspective on practice which arises out of very diverse circumstances and yet which seeks to arrive at a commonly acceptable starting point for local discussion. The reports provide an account of the dimensions of good practice, mutually defined across European countries, but they avoid prescription and highlight the ways in which the issues may be taken forward to suit local conditions. The discussion documents have been more useful in some countries than others, and probably least regarded in the UK, where it is very difficult to operate outside a prescriptive governmental framework. Nevertheless I would argue that they represent an important initiative in comparative research – within the definition of research I have been discussing as having both theoretical and practical outcomes. They have highlighted the richness and diversity of different systems of care and education, and opened up possibilities of mutual learning and development, the kind of cultural interchange Goldberger and Verkoff (1995) admired. (However, this is relatively easy to achieve in a European context where the dominant cultural groups hold a roughly equal status. It is far more difficult in Majority–Minority World discussions, or within countries where certain groups – for example, the Bangladeshi in the UK, or the North Africans in France, or the Turks and Serbs in Germany – are frequently regarded as of low status and threatening.)

I give an account of the second piece of sustained comparative research in which I have been involved in *Comparing Nurseries* (Penn, 1997b). This work arose through the informal contacts I had made in the process of producing the two *Quality* documents, when I visited nurseries in a variety of countries. I decided to try to compare the way in which three-year-old children were regarded and treated in local authority day nurseries in Spain, Italy and the UK. This study had a number of external constraints – the very different systems of provision; the funding which had to be negotiated in each country; and language. I speak some Spanish, but have only a rudimentary understanding of Catalan and Italian, and even with crash courses in both, I knew I would have to rely heavily on translation. This ruled out individual or group interviews as a method of obtaining information.

In terms of the general methodological goals of comparative research I describe above, I devised a number of levels of investigation. Firstly I tried to set the overall context in which the nurseries operated. I obtained documentation on the childcare and education systems operating in each local authority – bearing in mind that the system of local government and the relationship between national and local government was different in each case. (The Italians, for instance, have considerable local autonomy at a commune or city level as well as at a regional level, but a weak national state, whereas at the other extreme in the UK there is no regional government, and a highly centralist government.) I also obtained socio-economic data, looking at income and employment levels and other social need indicators.

Secondly I spoke to senior administrators, and in some cases politicians, responsible for the services, about the aims and objectives that had been set and the reasons for them. I also spoke to those immediately responsible for the service in the nursery – in the UK the Officers in Charge; in Italy the pedagogues responsible for each group of 10 or so nurseries; and in Spain the co-ordinators responsible for each group of nurseries. From them I also tried to obtain explanations about what the nursery was doing and why, and throughout the period of investigation I met with them regularly to compare notes and exchange views about what I had observed.

Thirdly, I asked staff to fill in a background questionnaire which gave me some basic details about their circumstances and their opinions about what they were doing. This was piloted in Italy, and hopefully was fairly translation proof by the end of the piloting.

Fourthly, I tried to live the life of the nursery, that is, to carry out ethnographic research as a participant observer, where I was there all day for a week (although unfortunately not consecutively or for longer, because of the difficulties of arranging meetings and translations). I watched the children, sat in on staff mealtimes and staff meetings, and on any other events that happened in the course of the week such as the visit of an educational psychologist, or a parents evening. I took notes of what I saw, and when the translator came in, once each day, and for any staff meetings or other events, I would try to ask questions as politely and as neutrally as possible about the meaning of what I had seen, particularly when it seemed unusual. 'Could you tell me why Maria sits by herself so much?' I would ask. Or 'Is it normal for Manuel to ride his bike through the kitchen?'

This method of participant observation demands a great deal of tolerance on the part of the staff. It is a highly artificial and often threatening situation to have someone watch you whilst you work. Whilst some of the staff, especially in the Italian nurseries, were very used to observers and to the idea of research, this was not the case in the UK nurseries where my presence generated tension. Ball (1993) has ironically described this kind of ethnographical approach as 'soft data and the skilful self':

> Not only do researchers have to go into unknown territory, they must go unarmed ... with no interview schedules or observation procotols to stand between them and the raw real. They stand alone with their individual selves. They themselves are the primary research tool with which they must find, identify, and collect the data. They must charm the respondents into co-operation. They must learn to blend or pass in the research setting, put up with the boredom and hours of an empty notebook, cringe in the face of *faux pas* made in front of those whose co-operation they need, and engage in the small deceptions and solve the various ethical dilemmas which crop up in most ethnographies.
>
> (Ball, 1993, p. 32)

In the course of the research I tried to encourage and answer questions from the staff as openly as possible, although doing so was not always straightforward, and it was necessary to view myself in perspective, as well as the staff I was observing. I was at one of the Italian nurseries when the Bulger case (two ten-year-old boys who killed a toddler) was being featured in the local newspapers. I remember a discussion with one staff member who was irritated by one of my questions. She told me firmly that they did not kill and persecute children as was the common practice in the UK. Given my background in such a child-hating country, could I be trusted as an observer? On a couple of occasions I saw practice towards children which seemed to me unacceptable, at least by my standards. When the translator came I tried to raise it with the member of staff concerned, again as neutrally as possible. If it was presented as normal I then raised it again with the administrators. One such example was of a male teacher preparing children for water play in the hot Spanish sunshine. Each child stripped, and then he smeared them down with sun cream, including their genital areas. Conditioned to accusations of child abuse, I was nearly apoplectic at what I saw as physically intrusive behaviour. But when I raised it in the nursery the response was 'the children used to be naked much more often, and even the staff took their clothes off'. When I brought it up with the administrator she merely laughed, and said that it was perfectly normal – and indeed chided me about it on a much later occasion.

After the data had been collected, and the observations completed, and after I had discussed my preliminary findings at a series of seminars and meetings with the staff, I tried to make sense of the data. I came to the conclusion that the differences in practices at the nurseries could only be explained by looking at the nurseries as part of the wider society in which they were located. Italy and Spain, or at least those regions in which I was working, were egalitarian communities who attempted to recognise the needs of all citizens, and saw children themselves as citizens or future citizens. So they had generous and well-resourced levels of provision for children within coherent policy frameworks. For example, the Italian and Spanish nurseries had well-trained staff who were able to review and revise their work through continuous training, with support from expert practitioners and researchers. This positive role and level of support transfigured the nurseries. It was expected that they would be sociable and stimulating places, the staff working would have fulfilling jobs, and they would enhance the lives of the children with whom they work – and in turn be enhanced by them. On the contrary in the UK the nurseries were part of a residual welfare service, a marginal service for poor children, and were physically grim places to be. In this context it was much harder to offer a fulfilling service, because so many of the odds were stacked against change and there was no wider context in which the work was valued or even noticed.

The differences in understandings about the role and function of nurseries in society in turn created diverse practices with children. For example, in the Spanish and Italian nurseries, the concept of a group of children, and maintaining the constancy of children's friendships within it, figured prominently as a basis for practice. Instead in the UK the fundamental assumption about young children was that they were individuals who could only learn in a situation which mimicked an idealised version of the home as much as possible, that is, through one-to-one relationships with an adult. Other children did not count; and neither did the daily organisation of staff in which the need to maintain high child–adult ratios took precedence over any need to maintain constancy of contact between groups of staff and children. In other words, becoming sociable and seeing oneself as part of a community were explicit goals in the Italian and Spanish nurseries (and indeed were stated as such by nursery workers) and the best nurseries had carefully worked out strategies for achieving these goals. In the UK day nurseries, there were no explicit goals at all, but the implicit goals clearly did not include sociability and solidarity and fellow-feeling amongst children.

I would have been unable to reach these conclusions had I adopted a more empirical methodology of comparing the incidence of certain types of behaviour of children; or their performance on certain kinds of tests such as ECERS (the Early Childhood Environment Rating Scale). The context and open-ended nature of the enquiry was essential to uncovering the differences between the nurseries; but in turn the methodologies I adopted depended on the prior assumption that childhood is not a universalistic phenomenon but a highly specific and local one.

Comparative research outside Europe

I have described comparative research methodologies in a narrow field, that of services to young children in European countries. Since this research was carried out, I have been carrying out consultancy/research in a number of Majority World countries (Penn, 1996; 1997a). Working in Europe has been a lesson in being open-minded. How much more so in countries where there are radically different understandings about childhood and where the circumstances in which children are brought up are so various.

I began by writing about cultural psychology as a possible framework for understanding how children become inducted into a particular community of practice. What has been happening, in ignorance of the precepts of cultural psychology, is that throughout the Majority World the concepts of child development – usually Piagetian, such is the time-lag – are being taken as universal, and (mis)applied with missionary zeal to societies and communities which cannot sustain them.

For instance, I recently visited Mbabane, the capital of Swaziland, where I was undertaking a consultancy for Save the Children UK. With the Swazi programme officer, I visited a number of informal nurseries which had sprung up on the edge of the city. These nurseries which are small backyard businesses exist in almost every large city in Majority World countries. In one nursery we saw the usual airless windowless hut that served as a classroom, where the children were so crammed against one another on the beaten earth floor that they could have been welded together. Incomprehensible charts written in bad English were pinned up on the wall way above the child's eye level. Most of the teaching was a chanting of mispronounced and idiosyncratic English phrases and rhymes. The teachers we spoke to were proud of their training from a local NGO (non-governmental or voluntary organisation).

By contrast in the yard outside there was a group of children who were not at nursery school (possibly because their mothers were too poor to pay for it) and who were unsupervised, or very loosely supervised. Whereas the children inside were cramped and immobilised, outside we saw children playing dressing up with a scrap of a kanga (wrap around cloth) and an old shoe – the cloth was used variously as a headdress, a blanket, a skirt and a floorcloth. There were some boys playing in a wreck of a car; and an older child playing a game with two tiny children each of whom held onto a strap tied around his waist as he towed them around the site. A woman peeled vegetables in the courtyard, with two babies alongside her on a blanket and one on her back. She chatted to another woman, and two more girls circled around them singing and talking in KiSwati. It was arguable whether the children were learning more crammed inside the hut with a minimally trained teacher, or playing outside it on their own. There were more dangerous objects in the yard than in the hut, and the children may have been safer inside. But in terms of intergenerational contact, and freedom to speak, and to improvise, and the expressed pleasure in what they were doing, the contrast was dramatic.

The net effect of the export of Minority World notions of early childhood development is an attempt to mimic received ideas about early childhood development without the resources (and to recite them in English or some other colonial rather than indigenous language). Most nurseries in the Minority World would expect to operate from inside a built structure which meets certain minimum requirement as regards safety and ventilation, and to have some trained staff – in the UK a minimum of two years post-16 for a nursery nurse – a requirement as to adult–child staffing ratios, a building, and a range of toys and play equipment to deliver the 'developmentally appropriate practices' which are said to stimulate children's cognitive development. In many Majority World countries none of these things are likely to be available and the question is whether they should be provided to the standard which is possible, however minimal, or not provided in this way at all. Woodhead (1996) has addressed this question in relation to schemes in Kenya, India, Colombia and France. He concludes that it is possible to attempt to provide such schemes, but that they should be judged for their quality contextually, by the standards by which children live locally. His view is that essentially it is acceptable to water down. Save the Children UK, a leading NGO in this field, in a recently published booklet *Starting Young* (Molteno, 1996) argue more strongly that the usefulness of many of the precepts which inform childcare and education is highly questionable. They argue this from the point of view of discussions of practical experience in many countries, rather than on the basis of theory.

This is a field which is only beginning to be explored, but when it does, it is likely to have considerable relevance for us in the Minority World. If young children can thrive under very different conditions from the ones which we take as normal, what does that say about the boundaries of our own child-rearing practices. Sensitive comparative research which investigates these differences has hardly begun (Pence and McCallum, 1994; Levine *et al.*, 1994) but would be of benefit to both Majority and Minority World children.

Summary

In this chapter I have reviewed some ideas about comparative research. I have argued that child development, which is seen as the underpinning discipline, is itself fragmenting and presents competing views of what children are and how they learn. Relatively recent work in the field of cultural psychology may offer theoretical and methodological approaches for understanding the diversity of children and childhoods, of 'the awesome variety of mankind' (Kessen, 1979). Such theoretical and methodological shifts are urgently needed. Whilst there is still a robust diversity of cultural experiences within Europe, the position of Majority World countries is much more vulnerable. Inappropriate Anglo-American models of 'developmentally appropriate practice' are frequently foisted upon such countries, in such a way as to override indigenous languages and traditions, and the rich diversity of situations in which children are brought up is minimised or overlooked. Comparative research has an important role to play, not only in recognising and valuing those traditions and situations, but in developing practice in early childhood services in the Minority and Majority World alike.

References

Balaguer, I., Mestres, J. and Penn, H. (1992) *Quality in Services to Young Children*. Brussels: European Commission Equality Unit.

Ball, S. J. (1993) Self-doubt and soft data: social and technical trajectories in ethnographic fieldwork, in Hammersley, *op cit.*

Boyden, J. (1990) Childhood and the policy makers: a comparative study on the globalization of childhood, in James *op cit.*

Bredekamp, S. (1987) *Developmentally Appropriate Practice.* Washington: NAE-CYE.

Bronfenbrenner, U. (1979) *The Ecology of Human Development: Experiments by Nature and Design.* Cambridge, Mass: Harvard University Press.

Cochran, M. (1993) *International Handbook of Childcare Policies and Programmes.* Connecticut/London: Greenwood Press.

Cole, M. (1996) *Cultural Psychology: a Once and Future Discipline.* Cambridge, Mass: The Bellknap Press of Harvard University Press.

de Vylder, S. (1996) Development strategies, macro-economic policies and the rights of the child. Discussion paper for Radda Barnen (Swedish Save the Children).

Elder, G. H., Model, J. and Parke, R. D. (eds.) (1993) *Children in Time and Place: Developmental and Historical Insights.* Cambridge University Press.

European Childcare Network (1996) *1986–1996: a Decade of Achievement.* Brussels: European Commission Equality Unit.

European Childcare Network (1996) *Quality Targets in Services for Young Children.* Brussels: European Commission Equality Unit.

Goldberger, N. R. and Veroff, J. B. (1995) *The Culture and Psychology Reader.* New York University Press.

Hammersley, M. (ed.) (1993) *Educational Research: Current Issues. Volume 1.* London: Paul Chapman.

Heath, S. B. (1983) *Ways with Words: Language, Life and Work in Communities and Classrooms.* Cambridge, Mass: Harvard University Press.

Jahoda, G. and Lewis, I. (1988) *Acquiring Culture: Cross Cultural Studies in Child Development.* London: Croom Helm.

James, A. and Prout, A. (eds.) (1990) *Constructing and Reconstructing Childhood.* London: Falmer.

Kessen, W. (1979) The American Child and other cultural inventions. *American Psychologist,* Vol. 34, no. 10, pp. 815–20.

Lamb, M., Sternberg, K., Hwang, C. P. and Broberg, A. (1992) *Childcare in Context.* London: Lawrence Erlbaum Associates.

Lave, J. and Wenger, E. (1992) *Situated Learning: Legitimate Peripheral Participation.* Cambridge University Press.

Levine, R., Dixon, S., Levine, S., Richman, A., Leiderman, P. H., Keefer, C. and Brazelton, T. (1994) *Childcare and Culture: Lessons from Africa.* Cambridge University Press.

Lewis, C. (1995) *Educating Hearts and Minds: Reflections on Japanese Pre-school and Elementary Education.* Cambridge University Press.

Lubeck, S. (1996) Deconstructing 'child development knowledge' and 'teacher preparation'. *Early Childhood Research Quarterly,* Vol. 11, pp. 147–67.

Molteno, M. (1996) *Starting Young.* London: Save the Children UK.

Ogbu, J. (1981) Origins of human competence: a cultural-ecological perspective. *Child Development*, Vol. 52, pp. 413–29.

Pence, A. and McCallum, M. (1994) Developing cross-cultural partnerships: implications for child care quality research and practice, in P. Moss and A. Pence (eds.) *Valuing Quality in Early Childhood Services*. London: Paul Chapman.

Penn, H. (1996) *Consultancy Report on the Mongolian National Pre-school Strengthening Programme*. London: Save the Children UK.

Penn, H. (1997a) Inclusivity and diversity in early childhood services in South Africa. *International Journal of Inclusive Education*. Vol. 1, no. 1, pp. 101–14.

Penn, H. (1997b) *Comparing Nurseries*. London: Paul Chapman.

Penn, H. (1997c) Cultural sustainability in early childhood projects. Paper commissioned by UNICEF for the Early Childhood Development Network for Africa inaugural conference, Cape Town, 1997.

Reinharz, S. (1992) *Feminist Methods in Social Research*. Oxford University Press.

Rogoff, B. and Chavajay, P. (1995) What has become of research on the cultural basis of behaviour? *American Psychologist*. Vol. 50, no. 10 (Oct), pp. 859–76.

Schaffer, R. (1990) *Making Decisions about Children*. London: Blackwell.

Shweder, R. (1990) *Cultural Psychology: Essays on Comparative Human Development*. Cambridge, Mass: Harvard University Press.

Stainton Rogers, R. and Stainton Rogers, W. (1992) *Stories of Childhood: Shifting Agendas of Child Concern*. Hemel Hempstead: Harvester Wheatsheaf.

Tizard, B. (1990) Educational research and educational policy – is there a link? Ninth Vernon Wall Lecture to the British Psychological Society. London: BPS.

Tobin, J., Wu, D. and Davidson, D. (1989) *Preschool in Three Cultures: Japan, China and the United States*. New Haven: Yale University Press.

Woodhead, M. (1996) *In Search of the Rainbow: Pathways to Quality in Large Scale Programmes for Young Disadvantaged Children*. Report to the Bernard van Leer Foundation. The Hague: Van Leer.

Young, M. (1996) *Early Child Development: Investing in the Future*. Washington: World Bank.

3

Early Childhood Education Research in Denmark

Stig Broström and Karin Vilien

Introduction

Since the end of the 1960s, early childhood research in Denmark has been dependent on individual researchers' personal interest in early childhood. The researchers have been mainly psychologists at university institutes or clinics for behaviourally disturbed children. A major part of the research has been related to behavioural disturbances, difficulties in upbringing and social disturbances related to events in children's lives, such as parental divorce.

Research in education related to young children is fairly new in Denmark, the first findings being published around thirty years ago. This research field is still limited in Denmark. The Institute of Early Childhood Education at The Royal Danish School of Educational Studies, which was founded in 1992, is the only institute in Denmark having early childhood education as its main brief. The institute has only five full-time researchers. However, early childhood research is also being carried out by a number of other researchers employed at different university institutes, by independent research institutes and by people with a personal interest in the area.

In Denmark more than 80 per cent of all children in the three to six years age group attend kindergarten and more than 90 per cent of all mothers of children under 6 years of age work outside their homes. This means that going to kindergarten is something 'all children do'; the kindergarten has in fact become a part of the education system, and this recognition has created the need for a change in the content of the curriculum.

To help the kindergartens and the educators cope with the challenges arising from this situation, there is a need for research in early childhood education. A new role for those working in the training institutes is that of seeking additional funding in order to dedicate all their research time to the field of early childhood education. It is probable that not more than 20 researchers in Denmark are funded to the extent that they are able to work full-time on research.

Generally speaking, two main types of literature on early childhood education are published in Denmark. These reflect the two roles of the kindergarten within a context of a rapidly changing society. The changes in society have needed to be followed up by changes in the curriculum, aims and values in the daily life in kindergarten. Thus parents and educators need the support and information available from different types of research. Educators are interested in the results of high quality research, which they use in order to secure the quality of education they provide for the children. Additionally, one branch of research is the traditional type, research conducted by an academic who is employed at a research institute. A second branch is development work, very often carried out by teachers from colleges for early childhood education or by the educators in kindergartens themselves. These two different kinds of research work result in quite different publications.

During the last three to five years, the main foci for traditional early years research in Denmark have been the following topics:

- play/learning
- care
- children as decision-makers
- children at risk
- developmental psychology and early education
- children's reactions to parents with alcohol problems
- daily life in care centres
- the transition from daycare centres to school.

This research would have been conducted by researchers employed by universities and research centres.

Kindergartens in Denmark see themselves as predominantly socialising institutions. They base their curriculum on play, genuine experiences and exploration in a home-like setting. Parents and educators put a high priority on independent behaviour and children's independent decision-making. The values described in the year plan which each kindergarten must work on, in co-operation with parents, are reflected in the research planned and practised by researchers, who have the right to decide the subject of their own research. These researchers very often publish their own research, often disseminating results in articles which often include information about the research process. Most frequently research results are published in books written for educators. In general research evidence is disseminated rapidly and is then used by educators.

Development work

Development work is mostly done by educators in crèches, kindergartens and leisure centres. Educators may apply for money from the childcare workers union (BUPL), from local municipalities (local authorities), from the Ministry of Social Affairs or from private funding agencies.

Since 1993, one of the responsibilities of the colleges for educators has been to conduct development work in co-operation with the daycare centres in their area. Some of the colleges are also developing research units in relation to this development work. The research units are funded through special research programmes, financed either by the government or by private funds.

This development work is planned and carried out in kindergartens by the educators themselves, sometimes supervised or supported by college tutors, consultants from the municipality or researchers employed at a university. All too often, however, the early years teachers are left to carry out the research unsupervised.

The content of development reflects daily life in contemporary kindergartens. At present this includes the development of:

- multicultural programmes
- play in the kindergarten
- the quality of children's lives in the kindergarten
- creative play
- care and education.

When a kindergarten receives funding to carry out development work there is a requirement that they provide a report, in order to disseminate their experiences to their colleagues in the field. However, this has proved to be too difficult without supervision, therefore too much of this valuable new knowledge stays within the kindergarten where the work was carried out. The exception occurs when the union magazine (*Børn og Unge*) has information about a project and sends a journalist out to the kindergarten to interview those involved. This kind of dissemination is very good because almost all kindergarten educators (95 per cent) are members of the union and receive the magazine. Municipalities which have funded research have started to publish their own results and distribute the findings; for example, through small booklets to all kindergartens within their own municipality. This means that in general research results are disseminated quickly and easily around the country. It must be remembered, however, that Denmark is a relatively small country with a high level of communications.

Government funding

Government grants for research are shared between research carried out by the universities and institutes and the research and development work in kindergartens carried out by college teachers and by the educators. The Ministry of Education, the Ministry of Social Affairs and the government Research Council for Human Research allocate money for research into early childhood. However, the government believes the greater proportion should fund researchers in universities, institutes and private consultancies.

This fundamental belief is the result of a philosophy of decentralisation. However, in practice it means that a significant proportion of a researcher's time is used for writing applications for funding. This year the government Research Council distributed 29 million Danish Kroner (approximately £2.9M) for cross-institutional research in early childhood education. The Ministry of Social Affairs distributed DK4 million (approximately £0.4M) among 31 projects. The last time the government Research Council allocated funds for this sector was in the period between 1980 and 1985. The Ministry of Social Affairs and the Ministry of Education allocate most of the money to independent research institutes, commissioning research into certain issues in early childhood.

Private funding

There are a number of private funding bodies in Denmark and most dedicate their resources to specific research areas or specific areas within development work. Projects using research money from private foundations are most often engaged in work on severe health and social problems, and the needs of children with learning difficulties.

Who does research?

The number of researchers in the field of early childhood education employed at universities and research institutes is very small, perhaps only twelve in the whole country. Researchers in education form the bigger group, comprising about eight persons, with the other four being psychologists. The remaining researchers are either employed in colleges or working as contract researchers.

The researchers in education focus mainly on children in the three to eight age group. Psychologists tend to focus on children who are at risk and the very young. There are, of course, exceptions. Some psychological research has investigated relations between children and adults. Five years ago, a large-scale project was carried out investigating how educators cared for young children. The latest project of this kind is focusing on children at risk and Else Christensen has published a large-scale research report on children's reactions to their parents' alcohol problems. Research in education tends to focus on play, children as decision-makers and children's independent choices.

Research methods

In Denmark research within early childhood education builds on several theories of science and, correspondingly, different researchers make use of a variety of research methods. As a result, some research projects are predominantly based on a positivistic scientific tradition, whereas others tend towards a phenomenological-hermeneutic approach and also to Critical Theory. Consequently, both qualitative and quantitative methods are common in the field. Although Critical Theory and qualitative methods are used quite widely nowadays, and are seen as perfectly respectable research methods, in general the positivist stance still dominates the field in Denmark. Throughout the 1960s, large statistical surveys were carried out in order to map children's growth. Questionnaires were used to investigate typical features of children's lives, conditions, health, schooling, development and educational achievements.

Irrespective of whether qualitative or quantitative approaches are adopted, researchers in Denmark tend to select their methods according to 'fitness for purpose', methods being chosen in response to the research questions they are trying to answer, rather than for ideological reasons. So if a researcher were trying to find out about or describe children's friendships, or to find what characterises the relationship between children and their educators (e.g. Thyssen, 1995) they might use methods such as participant observation, video-recording, interviews, etc.

Because many research projects in early childhood education have a comprehensive approach and aim to investigate and describe a variety of research elements, a conceptual framework incorporating different theories is often adopted. Among others, the German educational researcher Wolfgang Lafki has inspired some Danish researchers in underpinning their work with a critique of ideology taken from Critical Theory, a comprehensive interpretation of hermeneutics, and the collection of data by traditional methods with the idea of searching for causal relations.

To some extent, qualitative approaches might have been used as a bridge between the research of the university centres and the research and development work carried out by the educators. Researchers from the field of early childhood and elementary school could apply general ethnographic and anthropological methods (Hammersley and Atkinson, 1983). Shared methodological reflections demonstrate shared concerns – there are also some shared themes among researchers in the two sectors. While traditional researchers have elaborated their theoretical and operational positions in advance, some researchers have used an open approach, seeking grounded theory and adopting research methods chosen as appropriate at particular points in the process. An example of this approach is the work by Dencik, Langsted and Sommer (1989), which aimed to understand the modern childhood of the kindergarten. Through its open approach, this project was able to contribute new theories and concepts.

Concepts, assumptions, ethics and values

When children in schools or daycare centres are observed, interviewed or video-taped, obviously both parents and educators are asked for their permission. In addition to this, in early childhood research many researchers strive to establish an equal relationship with children, parents and educators. One might say that democracy, equality and openness characterise much research in the field of early childhood – or at least many researchers attempt to set up such an ideal.

Similarly, many researchers not only engage with educators and children as persons who deliver data, which the researcher uses in his or her own research project. Even when the research is not defined as action research or developmental research, the researcher often co-operates with the educators; for example, by sharing data with the educators. This enables a dialogue which makes it possible for the educators to reflect on their own practice. Further, the dialogue contributes to the process of interpretation. You might say that the possible authoritarian tendency in research is reduced through this kind of dialogue research. This is often expressed by the use of open and active participant observation – open because the role of the observer and the purpose is known by the children, parents and educators; and active because the observer interacts with the children, answering and supporting them. The researcher does not see the child as a passive object, but rather as a reflective subject. This means the researcher does not tactlessly enter into the children's world to observe them. As a rule the idea of the project is explained to the children and the researcher then asks them for permission. More recently young children are seen as persons who can provide the researcher with information more directly. In this way, child interviews are seen as appropriate and ethical methods. Here the big challenge is to remove a possible power differential between researcher and child in order to establish equal relations. For example, one researcher asked the children to choose the place where they would be interviewed. They did not choose the head's office but the top of a hill.

Correspondingly, researchers strive to share research data with educators, and some are also experimenting with returning the data to the children for their comment. Apparently the most successful so far seems to be showing the children extracts from video material taken earlier.

Links with theory

In general researchers set up their research design in accordance with their theoretical understanding, which most often is clearly expressed in their proposals. Thus the problems formulated and hypotheses put forward are in tune with their existing understanding of a topic and aim to add to knowledge and theory in the field. Some are keen to gain new insights into attachment theory, or Vygotskian theory. However, different starting points are clearly visible, such as institutionalisation being linked to lack of freedom; but on the other hand, children are enabled to interact with others through play and shared ideas. Early childhood researchers in Denmark do not share a common theoretical perspective, but it is possible to recognise that most research is permeated by a view of the child as an active participant in society with a role to play in democracy.

The Centre for Early Childhood Research

The Centre for Early Childhood Research is linked to the Institute for Early Childhood Education at the Royal Danish School of Educational Studies. On the board of the Centre a number of other research institutes are represented; for example, the University of Copenhagen and the Danish Institute of Educational Research. Researchers from different institutes can join in large research projects. The Centre also acts as a research unit linking educators and researchers who are interested in early childhood research but who do not have opportunities to conduct research themselves. At the Centre they become part of a network and they can gain research expertise under the supervision of experienced colleagues. A number of projects have been conducted under the aegis of the Centre, including work on:

- the quality of kindergarten premises in Denmark
- movement and music in crèches
- the issue of gender
- myth and tradition in the Danish Kindergarten system
- motor skills and development in toddlers.

Dissemination of research results

Research results are disseminated quickly to and in the field, because there is only a small number of larger-scale projects and public interest is very strong. Often articles are published during the research process and very shortly after a project ends books and articles aimed at educators will be published. In addition, the results of projects will often be made accessible to educators through seminars at which both educators and researchers participate. There are three or four major research journals and a few academic periodicals, some of which are aimed at educators. In general, research results are accessible to interested researchers and to educators in such a way that they can influence both theory and practice.

The impact of research on the field is difficult to assess. Results which point to the need for major expenditure tend to be ignored. For example, several studies have indicated that most kindergartens have too many children in each room and that this results in children suffering from infections and high noise levels. However, results such as this have as yet had no effect on legislation.

Qualifications and training of researchers in early childhood

Researchers in early childhood are included in PhD programmes at university institutes. The PhD programme in Denmark is of three years duration and includes a research project, seminars and work-shops on research methods, a teaching unit and a six-month study period abroad.

The PhD programme was started five years ago and the first PhD students in early childhood education should finish their theses within the next year or two. Most of those working as early child-hood researchers in Denmark have qualified through a number of dif-ferent routes, such as working at research institutes and participating in research seminars and conferences abroad and in Denmark.

Perspectives on future research in early childhood education

There has been very little research in the areas of curriculum, method and room arrangements. There is really no tradition in Denmark for discussing such issues. However, a new discussion has been going on for the last two years. The Minister of Education and the local admin-istration of kindergartens are supporting a closer co-operation between primary and kindergarten/afternoon care. At the same time, the school system in Denmark has been engaged in discussion about the teaching of reading with children in their early time at primary school. This is related to an international research project comparing reading abilities in grade 3 pupils (aged 9 years). In Denmark, this discussion now includes the kindergartens. The whole aim is to improve the quality of transition to primary school, as well as improv-ing the kindergartens.

In August 1997, the Institute for Early Childhood Education pub-lished the results of a large-scale project: *Myth and Tradition in the Danish Kindergarten*. Some of the results point to a need for research into didactics (teaching methods), especially relating to creativity, music and drama.

Connections to international research in early childhood

The group of Danish early childhood researchers have a close con-nection with Nordic and international research. During the last ten years Danish researchers have collaborated with researchers from the other Nordic countries and several shared research projects have been carried out. A growing number of Danish early childhood researchers have presented papers at the annual congress of The Nordic Society for Educational Research.

Danish early childhood researchers are also involved in international research and collaborate with researchers from other countries. Some participate in activities organised by the World Organisation for Early Childhood Education (OMEP), and through this they have established an international network. During the last seven years an increasing representation of Danish researchers has participated in the annual conferences of the European Early Childhood Education Research Association (EECERA) and, connected to this association, the Consortium of Institutions for Development and Research in Education in Europe (CIDREE). Since 1992 a Danish group has participated in three collaborative research programmes on early childhood education (e.g. Laevers, 1995).

Although early childhood research is limited in Denmark, many Danish researchers have published articles in international journals such as the *International Journal of Early Childhood*; the *European Early Childhood Education Research Journal*; the *International Music Journal* and the *Child and Youth Care Forum*. However, only a small proportion of the research carried out on early childhood education has been published – one might say this is the challenge for the future in Denmark!

Conclusions

The need for research in early childhood is growing and one main reason is that almost all children between the ages of three and six years attend kindergartens, which are becoming recognised as educational establishments. Thus, research on the learning process has become vital; so too has research on the early years curriculum, parental involvement and the length of the kindergarten day on children's development. Another important aspect is children's ability to concentrate with the large numbers of children in each group and the concomitant noise levels.

A little more funding is being awarded for early years research projects but it is far from what is needed. The lack of institutes with an adequate number of personnel who have time for research into practical early childhood education, with no prospect of this situation improving, demonstrates that young children and their education remain relatively unimportant to Danish society. Young children's education is still looked upon as the responsibility of the parents. The change in attitude needed will take a number of years yet to achieve.

References and examples of Danish research published in English

Broström, S. (1995) Education, motivation for learning and social competence of six-year-olds in kindergarten in Denmark and the United states. *Child and Youth Care Forum*, Vol. 24, no. 2, pp. 107–23.

Broström, S. (1996) Frame play with six-year-old children. *European Early Childhood Education Research Journal*, Vol. 4, no. 1, pp. 89–102.

Broström, S. and Vejleskov, H. (1994) Early childhood education in Denmark, in H. Vejleskov, (ed.) *Early Childhood Care and Education: 11 Countries*. CIDREE publication, Vol. 9. Dundee: CIDREE (Consortium of Institutions for Development and Research in Education in Europe).

Broström, S., Hännikäinen, M, de Jong, M., Rubenstein Reich, L. and Thyssen, S. (1996) The child's perspective – an extended view of what constitutes quality, in F. Laevers, (ed.) *An Exploration of the Concept of Involvement as an Indicator for Quality in Early Child Care and Education*. Dundee: CIDREE.

Carlsen, S. and Larsen, J. (eds.) *The Equal Dilemma: Kindergarten*. Copenhagen: Munksgaard International. (Contains chapters by Jytte Juul Jensen, Dion Sommer and Jens Qvortrup.)

Christensen, E. (1995) Families in distress: the development of children growing up with alcohol and violence. *Medical Research*, Vol. 54, pp. 53–9.

Dencik, L. (1989) Growing up in the postmodern age. *Acta Sociologica*, Vol. 2, pp. 155–80.

Dencik, L., Langsted, O. and Sommer, D. (1989) Modern childhood in Nordic countries: material, social and cultural aspects, in B. Elgaard, O. Langsted, and D. Sommer (eds.) *Research on Socialisation of Young Children in Nordic Countries* (Part 1). Aarhus University Press.

Diderichsen, A. (1989) Child development in a context of multiple caretakers, in H. Vejleskov (ed.) *Interaction and Quality*. Dundee: CIDREE.

Hammersley, M. and Atkinson, P. (1983) *Ethnography: Principles and Practices*. London: Tavistock.

Laevers, F. (1995) *An Exploration of the Concept of Involvement as an Indicator for Quality in Early Childhood Care and Education*. Vol. 10. Dundee: CIDREE.

Langsted, O. and Sommer, D. (1993). Child care policies and programs in Denmark, in M. Cochran (ed.) *The International Handbook of Daycare Policies and Programs*. New York: Greenwood Press.

Langsted, O. and Sommer, D. (1994). Modern childhood: crises and disintegration, or more quality in life? *Childhood*, Vol. 2, pp. 129–44.

Qvortrup, J. (1991). *Childhood as a Social Phenomenon: National Report: Denmark* (Eurosocial Report Volume 36/3). Vienna: European Centre for Social Welfare Policy and Research.

Ronnefeld, M. (1984). Children's aesthetic creativity – an indispensable dimension in a human society. *International Music Education*, Vol. XI, pp. 163–70.

Sommer, D. (1992) Children's living conditions, secular changes and childhood mythology, in *Educare in Europe*, Report of the European Child Care Conference, Copenhagen, October 1992. Paris: UNESCO. (Available from BUPL, Blegdamsvej 124, 2100 Copenhagen, Denmark.)

Sommer, D. (1993). A child's place in society – new challenges for the family and day care. *Children and Society*, Vol. 6, no. 3, pp. 317–36.

Thyssen, S. (1995). Care for children in day care centres. *Child and Youth Care Forum*, Vol. 24, no. 2, pp. 91–106.

Vejleskov, H. (1995) A study of children's acts and interactions during play with different play materials. *European Early Childhood Education Research Journal*, Vol. 3, no. 2, pp. 43–6.

Vejleskov, H. (1995) Dialogue and problem solving in children, in T. Helstrup, G. Kaufmann and K. H. Teigen (eds.) *Problem Solving and Cognitive Processes. Essays in Honor of Kjell Raaheim*. Bergen: Fagbok-forlaget.

Vejleskov, H. (1996) A pilot study on special application of the LIC-YC, in F. Laevers (ed.) *An Exploration of the Concept of Involvement as an Indicator for Quality in Early Child Care and Education*. Dundee: CIDREE.

Addresses related to early childhood research in Denmark

The Danish National Institut of Social Research, Herluf Trollesgade 11, 1052 Copenhagen K. Tel: 0045 33480800.

Institut of Local Government Studies – Denmark, Nyropsgade 37, 1602 Copenhagen V. Tel: 0045 33110300.

The Danish National Federation of Early Childhood and Youth Education, Blegdamsvej 124, 2100 Copenhagen. Tel: 0045 35465000.

The Danish Institut of Educational Research, Hermodsgade 28, 2200 Copenhagen N. Tel: 0045 31810140.

Centre for Early Childhood Research, Royal Danish School of Educational Studies, 101 Emdrupvej, 2400 Copenhagen NV. Tel: 0045 39696633.

Aarhus University, Department of Psychology, Asylvej 4, 8240 Risskov. Tel: 0045 89424900.

University of Copenhagen, Department of Rhetoric, Philosophy and Education, Njalsgade 80, 2300 Copenhagen S. Tel: 0045 31542211.

Socialministeriet, Ministry of Social Affairs, Holmens Kanal 22, 1060 Copenhagen K. Tel: 0045 33929300.

Undervisningsministeriet, Ministry of Education, Frederiksholms Kanal 21, 1220 Copenhagen. Tel: 0045 33925547.

4

Early Childhood Education Research in France

Sylvie Rayna and Eric Plaisance

Recent developments in care and early childhood education (since 1990)

As in most other European countries, the care and education of young children (aged 0–6) in France falls under two distinct rubrics: children over two come under the administration of the educational system, whereas those under three pertain to the system for child care. Thus two separate ministries, the *Ministère de l'Education Nationale* and the *Ministère des Affaires Sociales*, are involved, with an overlap for children between two and three.

Currently, 80 per cent of French women aged between 25 and 49 are professionally active. Half of children under three are cared for by their mothers (even when these are employed). The other half, whose working parents are unavailable during the day, attend crèches (collective, familial or parental), or are tended by professional child-minders (state-licensed or otherwise), domestic employees, or other family members. From the age of two, children can attend nursery school, but this is not mandatory.

Since 1990, there have been perceptible changes linked to the high unemployment rate, the deterioration of the economy, and the recent Law on the Family (1994), which favours keeping children at home or placing them with a childminder. Indeed, there is an observable deceleration in the establishment of crèches (whose capacity doubled in the 1980s) and a diversification in the supply of services towards more flexible structures, which are less expensive for the local community. Also noticeable is a rise in the number of *haltes-garderies* (childcare centres which, unlike the crèches, do not require that the parents be working) and the appearance of a number of innovative solutions aimed at community development, such as centres for free-

37

lance childminders (*relais assistantes maternelles*), or parent–child centres (*lieux d'accueil parents–enfants*) which bring together children and adults.

With regard to children over two in nursery school, recent changes have occurred more on the qualitative than the quantitative level. The attendance figures have remained stable for the past fifteen years or so (100 per cent for children over three and around 35 per cent for children aged two). On the other hand, with the implementation of the Law on Educational Orientation (1989), primary schooling, in nursery and elementary school, is undertaken in cycles regrouping several classes. Cycle 1, called 'early learning' (*apprentissages premiers*), concerns the lower, middle and upper sections of nursery school (children aged two to five); Cycle 2, 'basic learning' (*apprentissages fondamentaux*), concerns the upper section of nursery school and the two first classes of elementary school (children aged five to eight); and Cycle 3, 'reinforcements' (*approfondissements*), relates to the three final classes of elementary school (children aged nine to eleven). The aim is to provide better continuity in learning by tightening the links between nursery and elementary school – the last class of nursery school falling simultaneously under the first and second cycles. At the same time, anxiety has arisen over the loss of specificity in nursery school education (since, moreover, the inspectors for nursery and elementary school are now members of a single body), and over the increasing divide between nursery school and other preschool services. The programmes of 1995 confirm that nursery school is indeed school, even if the texts speak in terms of 'spheres of activity' and 'learning tools' and favour the construing (source: CNAF Action Sociale, 1995) and contextualising of these notions in a manner applicable to early learning. Finally, the creation in 1990 of University Institutes for the Training of School Teachers (*Instituts Universitaires de Formation des Maîtres*, or IUFMS), setting up university degree courses for primary as well as secondary school teachers, while it undoubtedly raised the honour of the school-teaching profession, also reinforced the fears we have just evoked (Oberhuemer and Ulich, 1996). The result is a marked distancing from the idea, originated in the early 1980s, of an overall and unitary policy for young children (Bouyalla and Roussile, 1982). The only official text encouraging the closer association of preschool services and professionals is a 1991 circular aiming to establish links between nursery school and other services and inservice training of a mixed nature is little known.

These recent developments have had their effect on research currently being done in the field.

Origins and current developments in early childhood education research

Contemporary research in early childhood education follows the path forged by a few pioneers whose thought is still very much alive.

A psychologist, Irène Lézine, holds a decisive position at the vanguard of research into the quality of education for young children. From the 1950s she worked, as a researcher with the *Centre National de Recherche Scientifique*, on infant psychology, in the wake of Gesell, Wallon and Piaget. At the same time, she was a pathfinder in the field of the 'psycho-pedagogy of infancy' (1964). Her educational proposals contributed significantly to the development of daycare centres and to their unshackling from the medical model in the 1960s, despite the general mistrust that reigned until the 1970s towards placing children in collective settings.

A contemporary of Irène Lézine, the psychoanalyst Françoise Dolto, whose interests included education and babies, may be ranked as one of the principal figures in the transformation of our relationship with the very young. Her strong media presence in the 'cause of children' (1985) found an echo among early childhood professionals, especially among educators working in *crèches* and *haltes-garderies* (Verba, 1994). With the creation of the 'Green House' (*Maison Verte*) in Paris in 1979, she was a forerunner in the development of parent–child centres.

Other researchers have also played important roles in relation to nursery school. But we must emphasise the part played even earlier by the women inspectors who, from the turn of the century, were introducing teachers to new thinking on the education of young children. The best-known of these is Pauline Kergomard, whose ideas were well in advance of her time and whose work continually astonishes her successors (Plaisance, 1996). More recently, a professor of educational sciences, Gaston Mialaret, has contributed to the elevation of the status of preschool education, in both the school careers of individuals and in school policy; for example, through an international report by UNESCO (Mialaret, 1975).

Other disciplines, too, have turned their focus on early childhood. In the 1960s, the seminal work of historian Philippe Ariès instigated a stream of important studies on the representation of childhood. From that point, historical interest grew, not only in the general theme of childhood, but also in those of birth, nursing and infancy (Gelis, Laget and Morel, 1978). Later, sociology also became involved (Boltanski, 1969; Chamborédon and Prévot, 1973).

Since about 1970, infancy has become a fertile field of research, affecting a widening range of disciplines. Psychology, especially, has seen a proliferation of studies on the perceptual, communicative and cognitive abilities of babies, in France as throughout the world. History and sociology, as mentioned above, have been joined more recently by demography and economics. In the pages that follow, we wish to detail the definitive aspects in the research of the 1990s, limiting ourselves, of course, to those works whose concern with education is explicit.

Early childhood education research in the 1990s is never immune from the influence of surrounding cultural values, which are also borne by the researchers themselves. This is true whether the research is being undertaken as a result of questions raised by earlier studies, or as a response to current social or political needs (e.g. the schooling of two-year-olds, the development of professional qualifications for early childhood practioners, or the prevention of illiteracy). In France, traditional values in relation to schooling are concentrated on the notion of equal opportunity. More specifically, they are concerned with social class and with the handicapped and not, as in other countries, with gender or race, which might explain the relative dearth of studies on those issues. Regarding the education of children under three, as undertaken by a wide range of personnel (*puericultrices* – nursery nurses, puericulture auxiliaries, educators, childminders, school teachers) and by institutional structures with a psychological cast, we can discern a recent trend towards a preoccupation with equity.

Nevertheless, on the level of the values inherent in different disciplines, we must underscore a certain diversity of perspectives, linked to whether the professional culture of the researchers is oriented towards the group or the individual. It is obvious that, traditionally, sociologists and psychologists do not approach the study of early childhood in the same way. At the same time, perspectives are changing. Let us note, for example, the transformation in the terms used to refer to the relationship between the child and the mother. The notion of 'maternal substitute' (a classical term used in clinical studies for the category of people who take care of children) is disappearing in favour of 'welcomer' (*accueillant*) (Bosse-Platière *et al.*, 1995). Although this term (first used for the staff working in parent–child centres) has a more positive connotation, it does not really evoke the educational function of early childhood professionals (from a fear of *'pedagogism'* – 'formal instruction'?) and no longer applies to nursery school staff, who are now officially 'school teachers'.

The choice of methodology, in connection with the intellectual field, is also very diverse. Analyses of documents, extensive surveys, interviews, more or less 'committed' observations, are all forms of action research associating the practitioners with the results, aiming simultaneously for the production of knowledge and the transformation of reality. Apart from their legitimacy in terms of their appropriateness to their object of study, these choices will reflect the value-systems of the researchers; for example, in whether or not they resort to a method that requires personal involvement.

All these factors determine, in part, the choice of issues in contemporary research on young children.

The principal themes dealt with today

The importance of the historical approach to the evolution of social definitions of early education and infant care is self-evident. It originated in France, developed by Ariès (1960) as part of a series of works on the history of private life. This approach reappears in historical investigations of the status of the young child in the family and in society (Rollet, 1995), or of the way early skills and learning have been represented over past centuries (Garner, 1995). And we find it again in histories of games and play (Brougère, 1995) and of toys (Manson, 1995).

The historical perspective also concerns institutions for young children – the crèche and the nursery school from their origins in the last century to their current incarnation, with a spotlight on the evolution of the social norms ruling them from within and without (Mozère, 1992; Dajez, 1994; Baudelot, 1992; Chalmel, 1996; Luc, 1994; Plaisance, 1994). Recent studies have covered the genesis and current evolution of new services such as parent–child centres (Eme, 1993; Neyrand, 1995).

The determining social conditions of preschooling have been examined from the angle of female representation in the workforce, or that of the evolution of the family, its needs and aspirations (de Singly, 1991, 1996). Some studies have been more particularly concerned with the social use of nursery schools and crèches, and with the expectations and attitudes of parents in relation to these (Norvez, 1990; Desplanques, 1993; Plaisance, 1994; INSEE, 1992). These studies have shown the expansion of the social use of these services (at first destined for the working classes) to all categories of society, from the second half of the twentieth century onwards. As stated at the beginning of this chapter, nursery school now accommodates all children aged three, while the schooling of two-year-olds is particularly prevalent

in the *Zones d'Education Prioritaires* (ZEPs). This involves establishments (nursery and elementary schools, as well as primary and secondary schools) situated in underprivileged neighbourhoods, to
which larger budgets have been attributed since 1981, following a policy adopted in the past by the United Kingdom. The monopolisation
of crèches by the middle and upper classes during the 1970s and especially the 1980s appears to have slackened in recent years (disadvantaged families had been forced to resort to childminders within their
family).

With respect to social history, recent studies of administrative policies for early childhood run in tandem with enquiries of a demographic nature (Norvez, 1990; Rollet, 1990). Moreover, French
researchers continue to participate in international comparative studies, following the one by Kamerman and Kahn (1981). Numerous evaluations of current educational policies have been undertaken.
Investigations into the functioning of the ZEPs have shown a perceptible improvement in student grades, class environment and teaching conditions (Liensol and Oeuvrard, 1992; Glasman, 1992).
Although investigations in the time-management of children's lives
(*Aménagement du Rythme de Vie de 1'Enfant* or ARVE) have demonstrated that this policy of expanding the interface between the school
and the community has affected nursery school less than elementary
school since the mid-1980s, and that the recorded grade improvements remain hard to objectify, nevertheless there have been perceptible changes, both in breadth and in depth, particularly with regard
to socialisation and integration (Burguière, Husti and Lantier, 1994;
Commissariat au Plan, 1994). Finally, studies dealing with the learning cycles have witnessed the dismay these initially caused among
teachers, but a recent enquiry into Cycle 2 has noted a net development of teamwork (Platone *et al.*, forthcoming). To finish, we note the
investigation into the working of the recent policy for cultural activities in early childhood (1989), based on the establishment of a partnership between culture and early childhood professionals. The
research has evaluated the pertinence of the policy and its concomitant practice, questioning its effectiveness in relation to the struggle
against cultural exclusion (Baudelot and Rayna, forthcoming).

The quality of early childhood education, the focus of numerous
studies in other countries, has not been explored in quite the same
terms in France. The question of the quality of nursery school education has not been tackled directly, perhaps because of the long-
standing and immense success of the institution, although concern
with quality of provision has existed in other forms since the incep-

tion of provision (Plaisance, 1996; Plaisance and Rayna, 1997).

Nevertheless, during the 1980s, a lively debate arose around the issue of schooling for two-year-olds and its effects. The results now available tend to demonstrate that this has had a generally positive impact on children's development in school and on their later achievements, although differences due to social class have not really diminished (Jarousse, Mingat and Rishar, 1992; Leclercq, 1995; Bemoussi, Florin and Khomsi, in press).

Daycare centres are now free of the mistrust with which they were viewed in the past. They are currently enjoying success as a result of their transformation, over the last twenty years, from stop-gap 'rescue provision' to contexts for living and learning. Indeed, the classic anxiety over the separation of mother and child is giving way to new preoccupations with the pathogenic effects of isolating children and mothers at home (reinforced by the phenomenon of social exclusion). Generally speaking, the effects of the various care services for children under three are being investigated in France, by comparative studies which use a variety of tools: tests, school assessments, observations in ordinary or standardised circumstances. Additionally, such studies now tend to explore the effects of different forms of provision on particular aspects of child development: temperament, language, etc. (Balleyguier, Meudec and Chasseigne, 1991; Cohen, 1995; Duru-Bellat, Mombrun and Tatre, 1995). A number of studies of this type are currently under way.

Psycho-pedagogical research, based on the theories of Piaget and, increasingly, those of Vygotsky, is similarly concerned with improving the quality of preschool education. Its goal is to find ways to unleash the full potential in each child. It centres on creating the conditions that favour maximum involvement in the co-construction of knowledge, among adults, children, and adults and children together. 'Interactive pedagogy', a product of action research in the fields of preschool and school education (CRESAS, 1991), is now promulgated through inservice training for teachers and other infancy professionals. Among the trainers are the practitioners who participated in the initial research. The cognitive and communicative aspects of spontaneous play in children under three have been examined in the context of childcare overall (Sinclair and Stambak, 1993; Bréauté and Rayna, 1995), both at the moment a child enters an institution and in the course of daily activities (CRESAS, 1992). Among the most studied activities of nursery school, oral and written language is the object of special attention (Florin, 1995). In France at present, the issue of the struggle against illiteracy is of great importance and the period in nursery school is considered a decisive stage in the acquisition of linguistic skills (Bentolila, 1996). Enquiries have been made into the efficacy of new technologies for language acquisition (Cohen, 1992). Also, cognitive education has been introduced, with the aim of developing meta-reflexive skills more generally, e.g. with the help of the American programme *Bright Start* (Paour, Cèbe and Haywood, 1996).

Innovatory preventive strategies (GPLI, 1992; FAS, 1994) designed to prevent early forms of scholastic failure (Plaisance, 1992) have similarly been analysed. Based on a collaboration involving many partners, these projects rest on the notion that intervention during early childhood can constitute powerful leverage for upward social mobility, and is thus a means of social integration. Examples of projects designed to investigate the bridging of gaps and to create equivalences between different forms of preschooling include that by Dupraz (1995). Glaumaud (1994, 1995a, 1995b) and Bonnafé (1994) carried out projects on early cultural awareness in a range of settings catering for young children, oriented towards those children and families most cut off, culturally, from preschool institutions.

The integration of handicapped children, present in the legislation but difficult to implement, is also starting to be an issue in research, notably in investigations of the collaboration between providers of special education and nursery school teachers (Vérillon and Belmont, 1997). A few experiments carried out by staff at crèches and nursery schools indicate positive changes in teaching practices and consequent benefits for the children generally, confirming the results of earlier experiments carried out in Italy.

The training and professionalisation of early childhood practitioners is an expanding area of research, with a whole range of different approaches: a sociological approach has been adopted in researching the training and work of teachers (Zay, 1994) and educators of young children (Verba, 1994); a clinical (Bosse-Platière *et al.*, 1995) or psychopedagogical one for the staff of daycare centres (Bréauté and Rayna, 1997). A number of action-research-training projects (Baudelot and Guibert, 1997) are converging on the interface between initial training and continuing professional development, the decompartmentalising of institutions, and the networking of professionals, in the wake of earlier studies done in Belgium and Portugal. Studies are also being undertaken on such new professions as that of 'early childhood co-ordinator' (Baudelot and Rayna, forthcoming).

Another series of studies concerns education in the family (Durning, 1988), a research focus that is growing in importance. Other themes being addressed by clinical researchers include that of 'fathering', following on from that of mothering, which is now being explored interculturally, as well as from an ethno-psychiatric perspective (Moro, 1994). This group is also interested in child abuse and protection, through action-research projects aimed at prevention.

Research policies: institutions and finance

Unlike other countries, France has no research centres specifically oriented towards early childhood, only a range of organisations which encompass research in this field within their sphere of activity. However, the researchers themselves have sometimes been able to specialise in this field and even to chisel out sub-areas, thus specialising in aspects such as the nursery school and its history, or language, cognitive development, etc.

Most of these are professional researchers, who generally have doctorates: university 'teacher-researchers' (*enseignants-chercheurs*, who have the double responsibility of teaching students and producing research work), and the staff of a variety of research organisations such as: the *Institut National de Recherche Pédagogique* (INRP), the *Institut National de la Santé et de la Recherche Médicale* (INSERM), the *Centre National de la Recherche Scientifique* (CNRS), the *Institut National de Statistique et des Etudes Economiques* (INSEE), and the *Centre de Recherche pour l'Etude et l'Observation des Conditions de Vie* (CREDOC).

In the universities, research is carried out in departments of educational sciences, psychology, sociology or history, but there are no units or centres specific to early childhood education, as there are in other countries. *Enseignants-chercheurs* are not required to be practitioners in the education of young children. The students they teach are not explicitly destined to become early childhood professionals, but the situation is rather complex: for example, some students in departments of educational sciences may already be professionals in nursery schools or daycare centres; others may use their university qualifications to apply for admission to the *Instituts Universitaires de Formation des Maîtres* (IUFM), and eventually become fully qualified school teachers, teaching in the nursery school sector. Finally, psychologists with clinical university training may also end up working, as psychologists, in daycare centres. It is important to add, however, the existence of inservice training on early childhood in some universities (Bordeaux, Paris), and a few rare new qualifying degrees in early childhood professions, in the form of *Diplômes d'Enseignement Supérieur Spécialisé* (at the doctoral or 'Third Cycle' level of university study).

Educational science, as taught in universities, leads to a degree but not to a professional qualification. As we have suggested above, a number of the students are already teachers, educators or other kinds of instructors, aiming for personal cultural enrichment which might, in some cases, be used later in their career, especially if they continue to the doctoral level. The professional qualification for teachers requires a candidate to follow a two-year course provided in the *Instituts Universitaires de Formation des Maîtres* (IUFMs). Candidates must already have a three-year first degree (the licence, roughly equivalent to a BA) in a choice of disciplines. Those with degrees in psychology or educational sciences do not necessarily have an advantage in admission to the IUFMs, some of which prefer to recruit graduates in mathematics or physics!

Up to now, research in IUFMs has not developed, insofar as the *Ministère de 1'Education Nationale*, on which these *Instituts* depend for the definition of their sphere of activities, considers the production of research to be the task of the universities. Nevertheless, the teaching staff at IUFMs include *enseignants-chercheurs* of university standing, who may be involved in research activities; for example, by co-operating with universities or by participating in university doctoral programmes. Nothing similar exists in the training institutes for other early childhood professionals, such as the instructors and practitioners trained in these schools, to staff daycare centres, for example. Tutors in these training institutes participate in research on a purely individual basis, either in education science departments at universities or by associating themselves with other research projects.

There are in fact no research centres specifically concerned with early childhood education, and research conducted in the generic centres can be external or implicated (collaborative), meaning, in this latter case, that it is undertaken simultaneously by professional researchers and by practitioners of education. At the *Institut National de Recherche Pédagogique* (INRP), many teaching practitioners are involved in research projects. In the field of preschool education, nursery school teachers and inspectors, as well as professionals from other early childhood services, are thus involved and trained in research. In other large research organisations, such as the *Institut National de la Santé et de la Recherche Médicale* (INSERM), or the *Centre National de la Recherche Scientifique* (CNRS), there are also some projects that include practitioners of education. However, at the core of these organisations – for example, for the evaluation and orientation of researchers and of research units – there is no specific section for 'education'. At the CNRS, for example, current studies in psychology tend to be directed at cognitive sciences. Education is nevertheless included in some of the research programmes of the CNRS, such as in the Department of the Sciences of Man and Society (*Sciences de l'Homme et de la Société*). Although this organisation recently financed a programme on the theme of 'Education and Training in Europe', not one of the respondents to its call for papers dealt, even fleetingly, with early childhood. Elsewhere, in May 1995, a National Committee for the Co-ordination of Education Research (*Comité National de Coordination de la Recherche en Education*) was created to conduct a regular stocktaking of research in the field, to compare it with research conducted abroad, and to suggest new projects and evaluate their success. We do not yet know if research in early childhood education will benefit from this.

Apart from the universities and research organisations, but sometimes in collaboration with them, projects are also conducted within or between certain government ministries. Within the *Ministère de l'Education Nationale*, the *Direction de l'Evaluation et de la Prospective* (DEP) regularly conducts a statistical survey of the school structures relating to provision for young children, and solicits targeted research; for example, on the schooling of children aged two to three. The *Ministère de la Santé et des Affaires Sociales* also conducts statistical surveys on the services under its administration (crèches, *haltes-garderies*, etc.) through its *Service des Statistiques, des Etudes et des Systèmes d'Information* (SESI). The *Mission Recherche Experimentation* (MIRE), under the *Ministère du Travail et des Affaires Sociales* routinely issues calls for research projects dealing with social security and solidarity, health, employment, and, less frequently, with education. In association with the DEP, it launched in 1993 a call for research on the 'education of children and teenagers', which would take account of the interests of families, educational institutions and social networks. Among the 21 projects selected and financed, five dealt with educational practices for young children and were conducted primarily by university teams including researchers from the CNRS.

Other research projects have been launched by a range of organisations with close links to government. Hence the *Fonds d'Action Sociale pour les Travailleurs Immigrés et leurs Familles* (Action Fund for Immigrant Workers and their Families) has regularly conducted projects related to early childhood, resulting in surveys, often in the form of local studies, on parent–child centres, intercultural structures, or the cultural awareness of young children, for example. The *Groupe Permanent de Lutte Contre l'Illettrisme* (Group for the Struggle Against Illiteracy) has also, for its part, undertaken a variety of surveys in the form of syntheses on the role of early learning in the prevention of illiteracy in young children.

Let us focus on the recent (1996) call from the *Caisse Nationale des Allocations Familiales* (CNAF) (Social Security Bureau for Aid to Families with Dependent Children) for research proposals. This call prioritised the following types of project:

(a) update studies on the effects of the different services on child development, with analyses of the scientific, ideological and normative discourses around the solutions considered most successful

(b) investigations of the various institutions and social actors now involved with young children, together with the resources at their disposal, and the rationale for, and differentiated effects of, their actions

(c) the interplay between the front line social actors (parents and professionals), their training, the dissemination of their skills, and the translation of these into distinct professions and roles.

Nine projects were selected to be carried out and four others were added subsequently. The participants are psychologists, sociologists and demographers from five universities: Nantes, Paris, Toulouse, Saint-Quentin-en-Yvelines and Poitiers, and professional researchers, from the CNRS, the INRP, etc.

Five of the projects are of the first type mentioned, in (a) above. Four of these are comparative studies (1–4 below), some of them extending the work financed earlier by the DEP. They cover:

1. the activities provided for two–three-year-old children in nursery school, in the various types of daycare centre, and by childminders, and the means by which these various professionals are guided; as well as the effect that the attitudes, gendered or not, of parents and staff have on the socialisation of children in terms of behaviours and language

2. the effects of the different kinds of childcare (mother, childminder or collective daycare) on the different aspects of language development (using films showing situations of children taking meals with their mothers)

3. an evaluation of the psychological development of 150 eighteen-month-old chidren attending different daycare services – collective (various types of part-time or full-time crèches) or individual (various types of childminder, in rural or urban contexts), including a

retrospective on a recent evaluation of 600 children aged between 10 and 30 months

4. processes of socialisation in the different forms of interaction between children, parents and staff in the different types of crèches (collective, parental or familial) among 150 one-year-old and 150 two-year-old children (using questionnaires and film)

5. a study of the evolution of knowledge and practices in care and early childhood education; this project will also explore the place of the father in the discourses developed over the past twenty years and popularised in the media.

Four of the other projects are of type (b) mentioned above. These concern:

1. an analysis of current changes in the educational models held by parents, and in their choices in childcare services, according to their material resources and their social and cultural levels (with a comparative study of rural and urban environments and a comparative study of different local policies in two administrative areas of Brittany)

2. an economic and social evaluation of the effects of different childcare services in the Nord-Pas de Calais region (with an analysis of the provision of services and of access to regulatory and interventive organisations)

3. a geographical study for the adjusting of supply to demand, cross-relating the geographical distribution of children and of childcare services at the community, inter-community and regional levels

4. a study of the place of early childhood in the planning and development of a new city.

Three more projects concern type (c). These are all surveys. There is a national survey on the profile(s) of early childhood co-ordinators and their role in the organisation of and innovation in childcare. The two others concern individual *departements* (administrative areas). One covers the parents benefiting from the *Allocation pour la Garde des Enfants A Domicile* (a social security entitlement for employing childminders at home) and the ways in which parents recruit their employees. The other deals with nutritional education for children under three and its relationship with the social and cultural environment of the parents and their chosen means of childcare.

Thus the financing of research can be summarised as follows.

Essentially, the financing comes through the universities and research organisations, whose contribution, in the form of salaries for researchers and teacher-researchers (who are civil servants), is very important. In comparison to what goes into salaries, research operations as such receive far less money. Nevertheless, freelance (or 'contract') researchers, called *'vacataires'*, may be employed over limited periods of time to participate in specific projects. The research proposals and reports are submitted for approval to the scientific councils of the organisations administering the research units in question. These quadrennial university fellowships or units of the CNRS are generally subject to complete evaluations and renewals every four years. But owing to the limited means available for carrying out particular research projects, funding is being increasingly sought from organisations other than those upon which the research units have traditionally depended. As we saw above, matching funds and co-financing are sought primarily when the call is launched for research proposals, but these rarely deal specifically with early childhood. A handful of private commercial enterprises grant funding for early childhood research. The Mustela firm, specialising in baby-care products, annually awards a prize for a completed research project and financial support for research in progress or at the planning stage. ASCO, a toy-making firm, supports the periodical review *Maternelle Magazine*. Two publishing houses, Nathan and Colin, hold pride of place in the publication of reviews and collections concerned with preschool education. They occasionally subsidise scientific conferences and events, upon application by organisers.

The relationship between research, policy and practice

The tripartite relationships that simultaneously involve researchers, policy-makers and practitioners are little developed today. However, at the beginning of the 1980s on the initiative of the *Secrétariat d'Etat à la Famille*, work groups were brought together for the first time. These included researchers from various fields, policy-makers from several ministries (Affaires Sociales, Education Nationale, Ville) and practitioners such as teachers, infancy educators and puericulturalists. They functioned within the framework of an overall policy for early childhood (Bouyalla et Roussile, 1982). Although this impetus was not followed through, innovations have emerged locally throughout France and it is on this ground that current initiatives, such as the cultural actions in early childhood, have sprung up.

What relationships are there between research and policy? These relationships are dialectical and exist on a number of levels. Policy-makers appeal to the expertise of researchers for assistance on specific points. Researchers were consulted, for example, during the formulation of the 1989 law on 'Educational Orientation' concerning schooling for two-year-olds, as well as for the programmes of 1995. Nowadays, they are particularly sought after in the struggle against illiteracy.

Generally speaking, policy-makers rely on the results of research, for the elaboration of policies which will later be evaluated, once more, by researchers. Examples of this are in the implementation of the *Zones d'Education Prioritaires*, of the *Aménagement du Rythme de Vie de l'Enfant*, or of the learning cycles in school which we described earlier. Thus, as we have seen, calls for research proposals are sometimes launched by ministries, who set the topics, and researchers are also present on the scientific committees of the MIRE, the CNAF and so forth.

What relationships are there between research and practice? Roughly speaking, we can say that there is little contact between academic research and practice. Early childhood is no exception to this rule. Of course, the resistance to change can be explained by the force of inertia throughout the different organisations, together with teaching traditions in schools, long-standing care methods and fear of 'pedagogism' (formal teaching) in daycare centres. The place of research in the basic training of practitioners is also open to question. There simply is none at colleges for *puericulture* (nursery nursing) and for early childhood educators. The place given to early childhood in teacher training courses is itself very limited. As for research in the IUFMs, this should be expanded in the future. Nevertheless, the new image of the infant that has been widely promulgated by the media – that of a creature cultured from birth, endowed with unimaginable abilities, for whom society has a duty to provide an environment favourable to the fulfilment of its potential – has impacted on the milieu of early childhood professionals (although not without distortion and abusive generalisation). The puericultural and pedagogical reviews available to practitioners have contributed, in some measure, to this image.

Nevertheless, direct access to research results, published in university collections or in scientific reviews, remains problematic for professionals other than those personally involved in action-research. When these latter become teacher-trainers, they provide an invaluable conduit for the dissemination of research results into practice.

In addition to the problem of access, there is that of disseminating research results, for no scientific journal specialising in early childhood education exists in France. Researchers generally publish in their field of origin (psychology, sociology, history). The *Revue Française de Pédagogie* is an educational review for general readership. However, we have just put together a special issue of this review dedicated to early childhood (Plaisance and Rayna, 1997).

We can thus understand the importance of courses of further training (organised by the *Education Nationale* for its own staff and by municipal administrations for others) or of the conferences organised by professional associations – the *Association Générale des Instituteurs d'Ecole Maternelle* (AGIEM), the *Association des Collectifs Enfants Parents Professionels* (ACEPP), the *Fédération Nationale des Educateurs de Jeunes Enfants* (FNEJE), etc. – where researchers may be invited to participate. A number of conferences have also been organised by municipalities in recent years and subsidised by the *Institut de 1'Enfant et de la Famille* (IDEF), on the theme of cultural awareness in early childhood (Glaumaud, *op. cit.*) as well as the range of events concerning infants and books organised or run by cultural associations, and created by psychoanalysts or by library professionals: *Actions Culturelles Contre les Exclusions et les Segregations* (ACCES), *Association Promotion de la Lecture* (PROMOLEC), etc.

However, conferences organised by researchers that are also targeted at practitioners are relatively rare. Nevertheless, we cite two recent exceptions: the Fifth European Conference on the Quality of Early Childhood Education, organised jointly by the European Early Childhood Education Research Association (EECERA) and by the *Institut National de la Recherche Pédagogique* (INRP) in Paris in 1995 (Rayna, Laevers and Deleau, 1996); and the conference on Cultural Awareness, Early Childhood and the Struggle against Exclusion (*Eveil culturel, petite enfance et lutte contre les exclusions*) organised by the INRP in 1996 (Baudelot and Rayna, forthcoming).

To this overview, we must also add mention of the important role played by international research networks. For many years, French researchers and research groups have been collaborating in international projects and publishing jointly with their counterparts in other countries. Thus, for example, the *Centre des Recherches de 1'Education Spécialisée et de 1'Adaptation Scolaire* (INRP) is involved in international research on babies in daycare centres, and has a long-standing, fertile liaison with colleagues in Italy and Switzerland. Other researchers interested in the history of education and of childhood have been active in the framework of the International Association for the

History of Education. They regularly organise meetings among specialists and develop co-operation with foreign counterparts, principally in Europe and especially in Germany. More recently, the institutional framework of the European Union has reinforced the possibility of cross-border scientific co-operation and encounter. Within this context, French researchers are participating in the following:

(a) the projects and publications of the Consortium for Development and Research in Education in Europe (CIDREE), in particular on research concerned with the quality of education for young children

(b) the activities of the European Early Childhood Education Research Association (EECERA), via conferences, the editorial committee of the review, and as referees and translators

(c) involvement in various research projects financed by the European Union, such as one dealing with the question of modes of supervision for early childhood professionals (the Leonardo da Vinci programme for the training of supervisors)

(d) the Socrates-Comenius programme of the European Union, run by the University of Liège.

A range of other international research associations have given space to early childhood issues, such as the International Toy Research Association. It must be recalled that individual researchers can also be invited to participate as experts in international labour reunions alongside educational policy-makers (for example, in foreign delegations to France from the USA or the United Kingdom), or in networks such as the European Childcare Network which was co-ordinated by Peter Moss. Moreover, these same researchers may be called upon to participate in conferences on early childhood, or to provide training courses in foreign universities, such as the USP in Sao Paolo, Brazil. Other projects of this type are being developed with countries such as Italy and Morocco. Early childhood researchers in France are, therefore, part of a growing global network.

References

Ariès, P. (1960) *L'enfant et la vie familiale sous 1'Ancien Régime*. Paris: Pion.

Balleyguier, G., Meudec, M. and Chasseigne, G. (1991) L'influence des modes de garde sur le tempérament du jeune enfant, in B. Pierrehumbert (ed.)

L'accueil du jeune enfant: Politiques et recherche dans les différents pays. Paris: ESF.

Baudelot, O. 1(1992) De la protection maternelle et infantile à la prise en charge municipale de la petite enfance: évolution des pratiques d'accueil dans les crèches, in CRESAS *Accueillir à la crèche, à l'école: il ne suffit pas d'ouvrir la porte!* Paris: INRP-l'Harmattan.

Baudelot, O. and Guibert, L. (1997) Métiers de la petite enfance ou professions 'expertes' pour la petite enfance, in S. Rayna and F. Dajez (eds.) *Formation des professionnels de la petite enfance et partenariats*. Paris: INRP-L'Hannattan.

Baudelot, O. and Rayna, S. (eds.) (forthcoming) *Les bébés et la culture: petite enfance, éveil culturel et lutte contre les exclusions*. Paris: INRP.

Bentolila, A. (1996) *De l'illettrisme en général et de 1'école en particulier*. Paris: Pion.

Bemoussi, M., Florin, A. and Khomsi, A. (in press) Scolarisation précoce et développement cognitif. *Psychologie et Education*.

Boltanskil, L. (1969) *Prime enfance et morale des classes*. Paris: Mouton.

Bonnafé, M. (1994) *Les livres, c'est bon pour les bébés*. Paris: Calman-Lévy.

Bosse-Platière, S., Dethier, A., Fleury, C. and Loutre du Pasquier, N. (1995) *Accueillir la petite enfance: quelle professionnalisation?* Lyon: ERES-CNFPT.

Bouyala, N. and Roussille, B. (1982) *L'enfant dans la vie*. Paris: La Documentation Française.

Bréauté, M. and Rayna S. (eds.) (1995) *Jouer et connaître chez les tout-petits*. Paris: INRP-Ville de Paris.

Bréauté, M. and Rayna, S. (1997) Diffusion des acquis de la recherche: une recherche-action par des praticiens de la petite enfance. *Revue Française de Pédagogie*, no. 119, pp. 5–14.

Brougère, G. (1995) *Jeu et education*. Paris: L'Harmattan.

Burguière, E., Husti, A. and Lantier, N. (eds) (1994) *Ecole et temps*. Paris: INRP.

Chalmel, L. (1996) *La petite école dans l'école. Origine piétiste-morave de l'école maternelle française*. Berne: Peter Lang.

Chamborédon, J.-C. and Prevot, J. (1973) Le 'métier d'enfant', définition sociale de la prime enfance et functions différentielles de l'école maternelle. *Revue Française de Sociologie*, Vol. 14, no. 3, pp. 295–335.

Cohen, R. (1992) *Quand l'ordinateur parle*. Paris: PUF.

Cohen, S. (1995) *De la crèche a 1'école*. Paris: Nathan.

Commissariat au Plan (1994) *Aménagement du rythme de vie des enfants*. Paris: La documentation Française.

CRESAS (1991) *Naissance d'une pédagogie interactive*. Paris: INRP-ESF.

CRESAS (1992) *Accueillir à la crèche, a l'école: il ne suffit pas d'ouvrir la porte!* Paris: INRP-L'Hamattan.

Dajez, F. (1994) *Les origines de l'école maternelle*. Paris: PUF.

Desplanques, G. (1993) Garder les petits: organisation collective ou solidarité familiale. *Données Sociales*. Paris: INSEE, pp. 330–8.

Dolto, F. (1985) *La cause des enfants*. Paris: Robert Laffont.

Dupraz, L. (1995) *Le temps d'apprivoiser 1'école. Lieux et actions-passerelles entre les familles et l'école maternelle.* Paris: Fondation de France.

Durning, P. (ed.) (1988) *Education familiale, un panorama des recherches internationales.* Vigneux: Matrice.

Duru-Bellat, M., Mombrun, J. and Tatre, S. (1995) *Les effets spécifiques des modes de garde et de la maternelle précoce chez les enfants de moins de trois ans.* Report of the Institut de Recherche en Economie de l'Education, January.

Eme, B. (1993) *Des structures intermédiaires en émergence, les lieux d'accueil enfant-parent de quartier.* Paris: CDC-FAS-Fondation de France.

FAS (Fonds d'Action Sociale pour les Travailleurs Immigres et leur Familles) (1994) *Petite enfance et politique de la ville.* Paris: Eres.

Florin, A. (1995) *Parler ensemble en maternelle. La maîtrise de l'oral, l'initiation à l'écrit.* Paris: Ellipses.

Garnier, P. (1995) *Ce dont les enfants sont capables. Marcher XVIIIe, travaillerXIXe, nagerXXe.* Paris: Métailié.

Gélis, J., Laget, M. and Morel, M. F. (1978) *Entrer dans la vie: Naissances et enfances dans la France traditionnelle.* Paris: Gallimard Juliard.

Glasman, D. (1992) *L'école reinventée? Le partenariat dans les zones d'éducation prioritaires.* Paris: L'Harmattan.

Glaumaud, M. (ed.) (1994) *Le petit enfant et 1'éveil culturel. Rôle des familles, rôle des institutions.* Paris: Syros.

Glaumaud, M. (ed.) (1995a) *Le bébé et les apprentissages.* Paris: Syros.

Glaumaud, M. (ed.) (1995b) *Plaisirs d'enfance.* Paris: Syros.

GPLI (1992) *Petite enfance, éveil aux savoirs.* Paris: La Documentation Française.

INSEE (1992) *Les enfants de moins de six ans.* Paris: INSEE, Collection 'Contours et caractères'.

Jarousse, J-P., Mingat, A. and Richard, M. (1992) La scolarisation maternelle à deux ans: effets pédagogiques et sociaux, *Education et Formations*, no. 31, pp. 3–9.

Kamerman, S. and Kahn, A. (1981) *Child Care, Family Benefits and Working Parents: a Study in Comparative Policy.* New York: Columbia University Press.

Leclercq, S. (1995) *La scolarisation précoce: un enjeu.* Paris: Nathan.

Lézine, I. (1964) *Psychopédagogie du premier âge.* Paris: Presses Universitaires de France.

Liensol, B. and Oeuvrard, F. (1992) Le fonctionnement des ZEP et les activités pédagogiques des établissements. *Education et Formations*, Vol. 32, pp. 35–45.

Luc, J. N. (1994) *L'invention du jeune enfant au XIXE siècle. De la salle d'asile à 1'école maternelle (1826-1881).* Thèse de Doctorat ès Lettres, Universite Paris I.

Manson, M. (1995) Jouets d'hier, enjeux d'aujourd'hui, in M. Glaumaud (ed.) *Plaisirs d'enfances. L'enfant, acteur de lien social.* Paris: Syros.

Mialaret, G. (1975) *L'éducation préscolaire dans le monde.* Paris: UNESCO.

Moro, M. R. (1994) *Parents en exil.* Paris: PUF.

Mozère, L. (1992) *Le printemps des crèches. Histoire et analyse d'un mouvement.* Paris: L'Harmattan.

Neyrand, G. (1995) *Sur les pas de la maison verte*. Paris: Fondation de France-Syros.

Norvez, A. (1990) *De la naissance à l'école. Santé, mode de garde et préscolarité dans la France contemporaine*. Paris: PUF-INED.

Oberhuemer, P. and Ulich, M. (1996) Les personnels de la petite enfance types de formation et offre d'accueil dans les pays de les pays de l'Union Européenne, in S. Rayna, F. Laevers and M. Deleau (eds.) *L'éducation préscolaire: quels objectifs pédagogiques?* Paris: INRP-Nathan.

Paour, J. L., Cèbe, S. and Haywood, H. C. (1996) *An Evaluation of the Cognitive Curriculum for Young Children: Effects on School Achievement*.

Plaisance, E. (1992) Un point de vue sociologique sur les actions de prévention et les institutions pour la petite enfance, in GPLI *Petite enfance, éveil aux savoirs*. Paris: la Documentation Française.

Plaisance, E. (1994) Les sciences sociales et la petite enfance. *Revue de l'Institut de Sociologie*, Université Libre de Bruxelles, nos. 1–2, pp. 69–84.

Plaisance, E. (1996) *Pauline Kergomard et l'école maternelle*. Paris: PUF.

Plaisance, E. and Rayna, S. (1997). L'éducation préscolaire aujourd'hui: réalités, questions et perspectives. *Revue Française de Pédagogie*, no. 1, 19, May–June.

Platone, F., Bouvier, N. , Belmont, B. and Seydoux, A. (forthcoming) *Les cycles pédagogiques à l'école maternelle et élémentaire*.

Rayna, S., Laevers, F. and Deleau, M. (eds) (1996) *L'éducation préscolaire: quels objectifs pédagogiques?* Paris: INRP-Nathan.

Rollet, C. (1990) *La politique à l'égard de la petite enfance sous la Troisième République*. Paris: PUF-INED.

Rollet, C. (1995) Le statut familial et social du tout-petit: aspects historiques, in M. Glaumaud (ed.) *Le bébé et les apprentissages: Genèse et incidences*. Paris: Syros.

Sinclair, H. and Stambak, M. (eds.) (1993) *Pretend Play Among Three-year-olds*. London:Lawrence Erlbaum Associates.

Singly (de), F. (1991) *La famille, l'état des savoirs*: Paris: La Decouverte.

Singly (de), F. (1996) *Le soi, le couple et la famille*. Paris: Nathan.

Verba, D. (1994) *Le metier d'éducateur de jeunes enfants*. Paris: Syros.

Vérillon, A. and Belmont, B. (1997) Intégration scolaire d'enfants handicapés à l'école maternalle: partenariat entre enseignants de l'école ordinaire et personnels spécialisés. *Revue Française de Pédagogie*, no. 118, pp. 15–26.

Zay, D. (ed.) *La formation des enseignants au partenariat*. Paris: Presses Universitaires de France.

5

Early Childhood Education Research in Greece

Alkistis Kondoyianni

Introduction: the historical context

Through the study of the history of education in Greece, in a socio-economic and historical context, it becomes apparent that when Greece gained its independence in 1821, after four hundred years of Turkish occupation, educational policy and the education system which existed were based on those derived from other countries, mostly European ones. Thus, at the beginning of the twentieth century some Greek educators who had studied at foreign universities and others, such as the inspired Glynos, Triantafyllides and Delmousos, became the educational leaders promoting change.

After having suffered poverty and ruin, caused by the Second World War and civil war, the country was struggling for survival. Priority was given to reorganisation and reform, but concern for education was put in abeyance. By the time Greece was being rebuilt, two phenomena dominated. On the one hand, many citizens, who were seeking employment and living very basically in destroyed or distant villages, were obliged to emigrate. On the other hand, others moved towards the big cities of Greece, thus creating astyphilia (urbanisation).

These consecutive social changes resulted in a crisis of principles and values. Once again education was neglected, the tendency being to adopt foreign schemes and patterns which were not rooted in Greek culture. Then, towards the end of the 1980s, departments of early childhood education were established in universities.

Thus, teachers colleges were replaced gradually by seven newly established universities in different parts of the country. Early childhood education was upgraded and what had been a course of two years of studies was extended to four. The Institute of Education of

Greece, in collaboration with the Ministry of Education, worked on a new curriculum for the kindergarten (1987).

The kindergarten teachers, who had graduated from teachers' colleges, updated their theoretical and practical knowledge by attending the Maraslios Centre for further studies (for a period of two years) and SELDE (Training for Kindergarten Teachers for one year). Later other educational centres, PEK, (Regional Centres for Further Studies) were formed. These centres offered training of a month's duration on certain subjects. Teachers had the choice to follow as many of these courses as they could.

During this demanding era, interest in education focused on research. Teachers and researchers developed their scientific interests in this unexplored area, in their efforts to understand the scientific character of education or to obtain a permanent job in a university. Meanwhile, technological institutes of education (TEIs) were founded, with the aim of educating teachers for infants, toddlers and preschool children (2–6 years old) and promoting scientific, educational research.

Over the last ten years many research programmes have been conducted, mostly by work in universities being granted financial support from the European Union.

In this study, because of the lack of a database concerning early childhood education research, we tried to collect our information from different sources. For this reason, the whole field of early childhood education research in Greece is unlikely to be covered – this study claims only to provide an introduction through which readers may begin their search and identify some of those who are conducting and publishing early childhood education research in Greece.

Examining the research which has been carried out during the last three years, the conclusion is that all the studies had certain features in common. Firstly, the research was usually carried out in the kindergartens. Secondly, the projects were investigations concerning the children, the teachers or the parents, and the researchers had an official permit given by the Institute of Education of Greece to whom they had submitted the proposal for the project, including its methodological approach, before starting the investigation. However, it seems that the parents had rarely been asked permission about their child's involvement, although most of the children, irrespective of their age, had been informed and had apparently accepted the whole procedure.

The use of quantitative and qualitative methods are used in approximately equal measure. As already mentioned, this survey showed that a wide range of research projects has been undertaken, surveys and evaluations being the majority. Comparative research, single case studies and action-research projects are less frequent. However, more recently there is a growing interest in action-research as a methodology and as a result teachers are themselves becoming more and more involved in the research and evaluation of their teaching techniques. Generally Greek researchers have favoured observation, interviews and questionnaires as research techniques.

During the last three years, the main foci of projects have covered three areas: firstly, the young child; secondly the kindergarten teachers, their attitudes, behaviour and training; and thirdly the kindergarten, the curriculum, teaching methods, educational policies, evaluation of programmes, etc. This survey has been divided into ten categories which refer to different subjects.

1. Educating the educator/adults education

In our changing society the role of the kindergarten teacher is also changing continuously. Many researchers have tried to investigate the motives for wishing to enter the teaching profession. They have explored teachers' attitudes towards different problems in the classroom, their beliefs, behaviour and practices as well as further education, alternative modes of education and training, and innovations in the preschool.

2. Educational subjects (research, policies, institutions and history)

In our country early childhood education is offered by two types of provision. Daycare centres, operate from 7.00 a.m to 4.00 p.m. serving children aged from two to six years. These are adminsitered by the Ministry of Health and Care. Kindergartens are open from 9.00 a.m. to 12.30 p.m. and serve children from four to six years old. These settings come under the remit of the Ministry of Education. Starting in September 1997, 160 kindergartens, named 'full day Kindergartens', started operating from 8.00 a.m. to 4.00 p.m. on an experimental base. There is continuous conflict between these two sectors and some researchers have tried to define the quality and the differences.

The national curriculum for the kindergarten was elaborated by the Institute of Education in 1989 and since then it has not been revised. Its application relies on the responsibility of special consultants, fifty people from all the regions of Greece. Some researchers are trying to assess different aspects of the curriculum, or to submit new proposals. Others are trying to define some problems that derive from the curriculum, or issues which concern preschool education today, such as, for example, the transition from kindergarten to the primary school and the new profile of the 'Europeanised' kindergarten of today.

3. Special education

There are many studies concerning special education, because there is growing social awareness of this issue. Further, the integration of handicapped children into ordinary schools has been started and is in an experimental stage. Up to now the teachers who work with children with special needs and rights have been educated through an additional two-year training programme in Maraslios College, but in the near future a new department of special education will be established in the University of Thessalia.

Furthermore, during the last two years the law about special education has been under discussion and as a result different studies have been conducted concerning not only special education in general but also teacher training, and the professional motives and satisfaction deriving from this specialised work.

4. Psychology

There are many branches of psychology which deal with the preschool age and cover several dimensions of developmental, social and child psychology. Research projects in this area often focus on socio-emotional development, the early identification of problems such as dyslexia, the psychoanalysis of group dynamics, the behaviour of young children in different situations, the role of the teacher in guiding this behaviour and so on.

5. Sociological studies

Sociological studies on preschool education appear more and more frequently. These investigations tend to have an affective orientation, focusing, for example, on self-understanding, self-esteem, the relationships between children and their families and with their peers, and so on.

6. Science (mathematics and physics)

Lately educators and researchers have begun to pay attention to science, mathematics and physics, exploring the effectiveness of different teaching approaches to help young children acquire an understanding of basic concepts and scientific procedures, as well as specific topics and phenomena of mathematics and physics.

7. *Language*

Language plays a vital role in the whole development of preschool age children. Therefore many studies have been conducted concerning this subject. Some have adopted a more practical approach and used literature (fairy tales, myths, stories) and language activities in the preschool curriculum. They have explored the connection between spoken and written language activities and other aspects of the curriculum, such as art, the process of learning to use written language, etc.

8. *Arts*

While the importance of the sciences is recognised, the arts are a significant learning medium in preschool. As well as their great value in relation to aesthetic development, they promote the intellectual, affective and psychomotor development of the young child at the same time as fostering the imagination and creativity. In Greece, the arts have captured the interest of the Ministry of Education which has been publishing books concerning this subject, in collaboration with the Institute of Education. These books have been distributed to teachers all over Greece. In addition, an arts programme, named 'Melina', in honour of our famous actor and ex-Minister of Cultural Affairs, Melina Merkouri, is being carried out in several schools of the country. Research projects concerning arts education mainly entail the development of art activities programmes.

9. *Sex education, environmental and health education, computer science and technology*

Several subjects considered to be the most contemporary developments in preschool education appear more and more as foci of research. These subjects include sex education for young children, though this is not referred to in the curriculum; environmental and health education – an area which is given a great deal of attention at present; and the use of computers and multimedia with young children, about which there are continuous debates and private initiatives. The Ministry of Education provides most support for specialised programmes in environmental and health education.

10. General subjects

During recent years there have been relatively few studies concerning general subjects, as there has been a tendency to specialise among Greek researchers.

The research reported here covers a wide range of subjects and has been carried out by both young and more experienced researchers. Due to the lack of an official system of collecting data this survey was derived from books and journals, from organisations such as OMEP (*Organisation Mondiale pour l'Education Prescolaire*), the Institute of Education, from technological institutes and mainly from the departments of early childhood education in our seven universities in different parts of Greece. However, this survey would not be complete without drawing attention to the real researchers – the many kindergarten teachers who are nowadays trying to combine theory and practice by being involved in action-research.

Bibliography: examples of early years research in Greece

1. Educating the educator/adults education

Alifieraki, E. (1998) The teacher's role in didactic communication. University of Padova postgraduate paper, 2nd Pan-Hellenic Conference of OMEP: *Postgraduate evolutions and perspectives on preschool and primary school education*, Athens, 23–24 January.

Anagnostopoulos, H. and Papaprokopiou, N. (1993) Further education and innovations in the preschool section. *Communications File*, Vol. 2, Paris: CNAM, March.

Doliopoulou, E. (1995) The motives for selection of the teaching profession by future kindergarten teachers and the factors which form their later opinion of their profession. *International Journal of Early Childhood*, Vol. 27, no. 1, pp. 28–34.

Doliopoulou, E. (1995) The motives for selection of the teaching profession by future kindergarten teachers and their expectations of their profession. *Researching the Children's World (Erevnondas ton Kosmo tou Pediou)* (scientific journal published by OMEP), Vol. 1, pp. 153–63.

Doliopoulou, E. (1996) Children's museum: an alternative way of educating teachers on the threshold of the twenty-first century. *Researching the Children's World (Erevnondas ton Kosmo tou Pediou)* (scientific journal published by OMEP), Vol. 2, pp. 11–24.

Doliopoulou, E. (1996) Greek kindergarten teachers' beliefs and practices: how 'appropriate' are they? *European Early Childhood Education Research Journal*, Vol. 4, no. 2.

Dragasi, E. (1998) Parents' schools (family consulting). University of Athens, philosophy department postgraduate paper, 2nd Pan-Hellenic Conference of OMEP: *Postgraduate evolutions and perspectives on preschool and primary school education*, Athens, 23–24 January.

Georgopoulou, A. (1998) Greek kindergarten teachers' opinions about their role and the meaning of 'professionalism' and professional satisfaction. University of Sheffield postgraduate paper, 2nd Pan-Hellenic Conference of OMEP: *Postgraduate evolutions and perspectives on preschool and primary school education*, Athens, 23–24 January.

Kaila, M. and Theodoropoulou, E. (1994) The ambiguous mediation of the none the less necessary educator: the case of the Greek kindergarten (*La mediation ambigue du pourtant necessaire educateur. Le cas de l'école maternelle en Grece*). *Perspectives Journal*, Vol. 26 (November), pp. 7–18.

Kaila, M. and Theodoropoulou, E. (1996) The educator and the drafting of the curriculum in kindergarten. Executing or co-founder? *Educating Community* (*Ekpedeftiki Kinotita*), Vol. 5 (January–February), pp. 28–31.

Kaila, M. and Theodoropoulou, E. (1997) *The Educator*, Athens: Ellinika Grammata.

Laloumi-Vidali, E. (1998) Educators' views on preschool education matters: preschoolers' involvement in the kinetic and mental abilities sector and priorities on general targets as well as on the organisation of programmes. *Researching the Children's World* (*Erevnontas ton Kosmo tou Pediou*) (scientific journal published by OMEP), Vol. 3, pp. 140–53.

Papagiannidou, Ch. (1998) Teachers and parents in preschool education. Positions and counter-positions. University of Lancaster postgraduate paper, 2nd Pan-Hellenic Conference of OMEP: *Postgraduate evolutions and perspectives on preschool and primary school education*, Athens, 23–24 January.

Papatheodorou, Th. and Ramasut, A. (1993) Teachers' attitudes towards children's behaviour problems in nursery classes in Greece. *International Journal of Early Years Education*, Vol. 1, no. 3, pp. 35–47.

Ramasut, A. and Papatheodorou, Th. (1994) Teachers' perception of children's behaviour problems in nursery classes in Greece. *School Psychology International*, Vol. 15, no. 2, pp. 145–61.

Vlachou, A. (1998) Education for everyone: educators' point of view on the process of the integration of handicapped children in 'normal' school. Sheffield University doctoral dissertation, 2nd Pan-Hellenic Conference of OMEP: *Postgraduate evolutions and perspectives on preschool and primary school education*, Athens, 23–24 January.

2. Educational subjects (research, policies, institutions and history)

Delonis, A. (1994) The school consultant today. Positions–Oppositions–Questionings. *Contemporary School* (*Synchrono Scholio*), Vol. 23, pp. 177–81.

Huttugen, E. (1994) Children's experience of the early childhood education programmes. *Contemporary Kindergarten* (*Synchrono Nipiagogio*), Vol. 21–22, pp. 144–6.

Kaila, M. and Theodoropoulou, E. (1995) Curricula in general education, with emphasis on preschool age: speculations and perspectives. Proceedings of the Pan-Hellenic Pedagogical Conference: 'Curricula in General Education and Teachers Training. Theory and Practice'. Editions of the educational institute *PLATON*, pp. 163–80.

Kakavoulis, A. (1993) The role of the daycare centre and the nursery school in cognitive, social and emotional development of the child. *Ellinochristianiki Agogi* (Greek Orthodox education journal), Vol. 405, pp. 261–8 and Vol. 406, pp. 296–300.

Kakavoulis, A. (1994) Continuity in early childhood education: transition from preschool to school. *International Journal of Early Years Education*, Vol. 2, no. 1, Spring, pp. 41–51.

Koffas, A. and Metohiannakis, H. (1994) *Basic Problems in Preschool Education. an Empirical Pedagogical Approach to Kindergarten Problems*. University of Rethymno.

Papaprokopiou, N. (1995) Pedagogy of contrasts. introduction to the banquet. *Training the preschool age child*. Athens: Preschool Centre of Bank of Greece.

Petrogiannis, K. and Melhuish, E. C. (1996) Aspects of quality in Greek day-care centres. *European Journal of Psychology of Education*, Vol. 11, no. 2, pp. 177–91.

Polychronopoulos, P. (1996) Towards a new attestation and formation of kindergarten curriculum. *Researching the Children's World (Erevnondas ton Kosmo tou Pediou)* (scientific journal published by OMEP), Vol. 2, pp. 25–45.

Zacharenakis, K. (1995) Pedagogical and political organisation of 'European schools' (research approach). *Researching the Children's World (Erevnondas ton Kosmo tou Pediou)* (scientific journal published by OMEP), Vol. 1, pp. 164–74.

3. Special education

Anagnostopoulos, H., Boada, R., Torres, M. and Verillion, A. (1993) *Social integration of handicapped children. Innovating actions in the preschool education: key factors and perspectives. Report for the European Commission*. Paris: IEDPE, September.

Anagnostopoulos, H. (1994) The integration of young handicapped children in normal day nurseries: teachers' views. *The Handicapped (I anapiri)*, Vol. B, Athens: Ellinika Grammata editions.

Charitou, S. (1998) Natural science and mental retardment: the didactic programme by Copple, Sigel and Sanders adjusted for children facing learning disabilities. University of Athens postgraduate paper, 2nd Pan-Hellenic Conference of OMEP: *Postgraduate evolutions and perspectives on preschool and primary school education*, Athens, 23–24 January.

Deropoulou-Derou, E. (1998) Abilities of understanding of various forms of speech by preschool aged children facing hearing problems, during their education. Lenin University of Moscow postgraduate paper, 2nd Pan-Hellenic Conference of OMEP: *Postgraduate evolutions and perspectives on preschool and primary school education*, Athens, 23–24 January.

Giannousa, P., Moulavasili, A. and Bezeritzoglou, M. (1997) The integration of handicapped children in normal nurseries: the teachers' views. 6th Pan-Hellenic Seminar of Preschool Educators (TEI): *Communication in the preschool age: conditions for development*, Athens, 29–30 November.

Karayianni, Y. (1998) Evaluating an educational unit (language unit) for children with language disorders: its role in the integration process. University of Birmingham postgraduate paper, 2nd Pan-Hellenic Conference of OMEP: *Postgraduate evolutions and perspectives on preschool and primary school education*, Athens, 23–24 January.

Koutsogianni, I., Kremiotou, D. and Lagiou, M. (1997) The integration of handicapped children in normal institutions: the attitude of parents of normal children. 6th Pan-Hellenic Seminar of Preschool Educators (TEI): *Communication in the preschool age: conditions for development*, Athens, 29–30 November.

Stavrou, I. and Bonia, A. (1994) A case study: a trial of training and incorporation in the school peer of a four-year-old blind and autistic child. University of Ioannina, Department of Preschool Education, Workshop of Special and Remedial Education.

Stavrou, L. and Christoforidou, K. (1995) A multi-factored approach of basic professional training and formation process of teachers of special education in Greece. University of Ioannina, Department of Preschool Education, Workshop of Special and Remedial Education.

Stavrou, L. and Christoforidou, K. (1996) The profile of the personnel that frames the Greek special classes and schools. University of Ioannina, Department of Preschool Education, Workshop of Special and Remedial Education.

Stavrou, L. and Christoforidou, K. (1995) Motives and professional satisfaction of teachers who frame the special classes and special schools in Greece. University of Ioannina, Department of Preschool Education, Workshop of Special and Remedial Education.

Stavrou, L. (1996) The playing and the remedy of corporal scheme concerning the child with spastic cerebral palsy. University of Ioannina, Department of Preschool Education, Workshop of Special and Remedial Education.

Stavrou, L. and Sarris, D. (1996) Corporal scheme and body image concerning people with spastic cerebral palsy. University of Ioannina, Department of Preschool Education, Workshop of Special and Remedial Education and UFR de Psychologie et des Sciences de l'Education, Laboratoire EURED, Université de Toulouse-Le Mirail, France.

Theodorou, E. (1994) The integration of deaf children in kindergarten. *Open School (Anihto Scholio)*, Vol. 50, pp. 9–11.

Vitsentou, Ch., Gatsiou, S. and Karamani, L. (1997) The integration of handicapped children in normal nurseries: their parents' views and attitude. 6th Pan-Hellenic Seminar of Preschool Educators (TEI): *Communication in the preschool age: conditions for development*, Athens, 29–30 November.

4. *Psychology*

Dereka, M. (1998) Writing problems of children facing learning problems. University of Sheffield postgraduate paper, 2nd Pan-Hellenic Conference of OMEP: *Postgraduate evolutions and perspectives on preschool and primary school education*, Athens, 23–24 January.

Hatzichristou, Ch. (1995) Pupils with special demands in primary education: difficulties in school and the role of the school psychologist. *Researching the Children's World (Erevnondas ton Kosmo tou Pediou)* (scientific journal published by OMEP), Vol. 1, pp. 68–76.

Kaila, M., Polemikos, N. and Ksanthakou, G. (1996) *School Phobia*. Athens: Ellinika Grammata.

Kaila, M. and Tsambarlis, A. (1995) The pariah in the classroom, in *School Failure*. Athens: Ellinika Grammata.

Kakavoulis, A. (1993) Psychological adjustment of children in nursery school. *Pedagogical Review (Pedagogiki Epitheorisi)*, Vol. 18, pp. 63–81.

Kakavoulis, A. (1994) Psychological maturity of children for their entrance to primary school and the role of nursery school. Conference of Preschool Education, University of Ioannina, May.

Kakavoulis, A. (1995) The concept of good and evil in children of preschool age. *Researching the Children's World (Erevnondas ton Kosmo tou Pediou)* (scientific journal published by OMEP), Vol. 1, pp. 77–87.

Kakavoulis, A. (1996) Aggressive and anti-social behaviour in young Greek children. 2nd International Early Years Conference, University of Warwick, March.

Karathanasi-Katsaounou, A. (1998) Children's jealousy. *Researching the Children's World (Erevnondas ton kosmo tou Pediou)* (scientific journal published by OMEP), Vol. 3, pp. 186–205.

Kondoyianni, A. (1997) Affective education in Greece: the self-understanding of preschool children as projected by puppets. *OMEP International Journal*, Vol. 29, no. 1, pp. 10–18.

Malikiosi-Loizou, M. (1994) The advisory orientation functionary in the bounds of preschool education: role–targets–personality–abilities. *Advisory–Orientation Review (Simvouleftikos prosanatolismos)*, Vol. 30–31, pp. 101–6.

Malikiosi-Loizou, M. (1996) The importance of advisory in preschool education. 5th Pan-Hellenic Conference of Psychological Research, Patra, May.

Martsinkofskagia, T. (1995) Social emotions and their development in preschool age. *Educating Community (Ekpedeftiki Kinotita)*, Vol. 30, pp. 24–7.

Petrogiannis, K. (1998) Psychological development at 18 months of age as a function of childcare experience in Greece. Doctoral dissertation, University of Wales, College of Cardiff, 2nd Pan-Hellenic Preschool Conference of OMEP, 23–25 January.

Petrogiannis, K. G. and Melhuish, E. C. (1996) Socio-emotional development at 18 months of age in relation to the quality of care at home and in day-care in Greece. XIVth Biennial Meeting of the International Society for the

Study of Behavioral Development, Quebec City, Canada, 12–16 August.

Stavrou, L. (1995) A study of socio-therapeutic group dynamics. University of Ioannina, Department of Preschool Education, Workshop of Special and Remedial Education.

Stavrou, L. (1997) Phycho-therapeutic relation and psychoanalytical approach of kindergarten class dynamics. University of Ioannina, Department of Preschool Education, Workshop of Special and Remedial Education.

Stavrou, L. and Sarris, D. (1996) The construction of space and father figure through the projective technique of the 'village' (*test du village*). University of Ioannina, Department of Preschool Education, Workshop of Special and Remedial Education and UFR de Psychologie et des Sciences de l'Education, Laboratoire EURED, Universite de Toulouse-Le Mirail, France.

Stavrou, L. (1996) Early identification of tendencies to dyslexia and remedy at kindergarten and primary school. University of Ioannina, Department of Preschool Education, Workshop of Special and Remedial Education.

Stavrou, L. and Zakopoulou, V. (1996) Content analysis of dyslexic children's texts at school, in Ioannina's area. University of Ioannina, Department of Preschool Education, Workshop of Special and Remedial Education.

Stavrou, L. and Zakopoulou, V. (1995) Early identification of tendencies to dyslexia at preschool age. University of Ioannina, Department of Preschool Education, Workshop of Special and Remedial Education.

Tsiliki, F. (1996) How do children distinguish between irony and deception and how they understand the behaviour and the profound intentions of the ironist and the deceiver. *Researching the Children's World* (*Erevnondas ton Kosmo tou Pediou*) (scientific journal published by OMEP), Vol. 2, pp. 95–105.

Vagenas, E. (1995) The role of the kindergarten teacher in the aggressive behaviour of preschool age children. *Researching the Children's World* (*Erevnondas ton Kosmo tou Pediou*) (scientific journal published by OMEP), Vol. 1, pp. 88–98.

Varvogli, L. (1998) Psychological influences of earthquakes on children and ways to cope with them. *Researching the Children's World* (*Erevnondas ton kosmo tou Pediou*) (scientific journal published by OMEP), Vol. 3, pp. 179–85.

5. Sociological subjects

Bellas, Th. (1995) Equality of the sexes in the educational process: prejudices and reality, in *Inter-sex relations*, Vol. 1. Athens: Ellinika Grammata.

Doliopoulou, E. (1995) Social studies as a form and medium of education in the Greek kindergarten. *International Journal of Early Years Education*, Vol. 3, no. 2, pp. 47–61.

Doulkeris, T., Ioannides, M.,-Kagiafa, A. and Loupakis, I. (1996) Stereotypes of the two sexes in the media for children, in *Inter-sex relations*, Vol. 2, Athens: Ellinika Grammata.

Kakavoulis, A. (1996) Early childhood altruism: how parents see pre-social behaviour of their young children. International Conference of the Institute of Educational Research, Belgrade, October.

Laloumi-Vidali, E. (1997) Professional views on parents' involvement at the partnership level in preschool education. *International Journal of Early Childhood Education,* Vol. 29, no. 1, pp. 19–25.

Leontitsis-Giannis, E. (1995) The role of the Greek father in the upbringing of children. *Educating Community (Ekpedeftiki Kinotita),* Vol. 30, pp. 32–4.

Malikiosi-Loizou, M. (1995) Inter-generation relations and notions: First and Third age. *Researching the Children's World (Erevnondas ton Kosmo tou Pediou)* (scientific journal published by OMEP), Vol. 1, pp. 51–67.

Malikiosi-Loizou, M. (1996) Inter-generation relations: facts and principles of communication and solidarity. Proceedings of EKKE's Pan-Hellenic Conference: *Growing Old and Society,* pp. 387–400.

Malikiosi-Loizou, M. (1996) Advantages and disadvantages of the elderly's presence in the family. 8th International Conference of the International Association for Family Treatment, Athens, July

Paraskevopoulou, M. (1997) We opened the door and...we met with life. 6th Pan-Hellenic Seminar of Preschool Educators (TEI): *Communication in the preschool age: conditions for development,* Athens, 29–30 November.

6. Science (mathematics and physics)

Charalambopoulou, C., Cosmopoulou, D., Ravanis, K. and Papamichael, Y. (submitted for publication) The formation of shadows: a didactic intervention for the destabilisation of mental representations of children of preschool age. University of Patras.

Doliopoulou, E. (1994) Mathematics as a form and medium of education in the Greek kindergarten. *European Early Childhood Education Research Journal,* Vol. 2, no. 1, pp. 61–78.

Galimitaki, D., Karamanou, A., Kordistou, M., Barbayianni, E., Pappa, E. and Ravanis, K. (1995) Natural science in preschool education: the example of the initiation to magnetism. *Contemporary Education (Synchroni Ekpedefsi),* Vol. 81, pp. 85–91.

Hatzinikita, V., Koulaidis, V. and Ravanis, K. (1996) Ideas of preschool and first school age children about the boiling of water. *Researching the Children's World (Erevnondas ton Kosmo tou Pediou)* (scientific journal published by OMEP), Vol. 2, pp. 106–16.

Ioannides, C. and Kakana, D. M. (1996) Promoting the understanding of the floating of objects in kindergarten children. International conference, 'The growing mind', University of Geneva, 14–18 September.

Kakana, D. M. (1997) The construction of space in kindergarten children: the effects of an instructional intervention. 7th European Conference for Research on Learning and Instruction (EARLI), Athens, 26–30 August.

Kiehagia, I., Mati, S. and Mermyga, E. (1995) Education of the sense of time in infants. 5th Pan-Hellenic Seminar of Preschool Educators (TEI): *Contemporary pedagogical approach,* Thessaloniki, 25–26 November.

Kokkotas, P. (1995) Scientific procedures and basic concepts of natural science in the kindergarten curriculum: the sense of movement as understood by children 5–6 years of age. *Researching the Children's World (Erevnondas ton Kosmo tou Pediou)* (scientific journal published by OMEP), Vol. 1, pp. 11–17.

Papandreou, M. (1998) The learning process of the first mathematical concepts: length, distance, measurement. University of Aix-Marseille postgraduate paper, 2nd Pan-Hellenic Conference of OMEP: *Postgraduate evolutions and perspectives on preschool and primary school education*, Athens, 23–24 January.

Poulos, A. (1994) Pedagogical intervention in the formation of concepts of the geometrical space in preschool age children. Doctoral dissertation, University of Thessaloniki, Department of Preschool Education.

Ravanis, K. (1994) Curriculum and science education: the case of preschool age. Pan-Hellenic conference, Curricula in Preschool Education. Department of Preschool Education, University of Ioannina, Ioannina 20–22 May.

Ravanis, K. and Bagakis, G. (1995) Towards integration of science education in preschool education. European Conference on Research in Science Education, University of Leeds, Leeds, 7–11 April.

Ravanis, K. (1996) Didactic intervention strategies for the initiation of preschool age children in science (*Strategies d'interventions didactiques pour l'initiation des enfants de l'école maternelle en sciences physiques*). *Revue de Recherches en Education: Spirale*, Vol. 17, pp. 161–76.

Ravanis, K. (1995) The formation of shadows: conflicting didactic procedures (*La formation des ombres: procedures didactiques conflictuelles*). Colloque franco-quebecois, *La Tutelle en Sciences Experimentales*, Université Paris VII-Denis Diderot, Paris, 2–3 Mars.

Ravanis, K. (1994) The discovery of elementary magnetic properties in preschool age: a qualitative and quantitative research within a Piagetian framework. *European Early Childhood Education Research*, Vol. 2, no. 2, pp. 79–91.

Ravanis, K. (1995) The concept of the light: representations of five-year-old children. (*Le concept de lumière: representations des enfants de cinq ans*). 5th European Congress on the Quality of Education of Young Children. What pedagogical objectives for the preschool education (0–7 years of age) INRP–EECERA, Sorbonne, Paris, 7–9 September.

Tjekaki, M. and Kalaitjidou, S. (1998) A research programme for the development of the first mathematical concepts. *Researching the Children's World (Erevnondas ton kosmo tou Pediou)* (scientific journal published by OMEP), Vol. 3, pp. 72–83.

Vaitsi, M., Papageorgiou, V., Bagakis, G., Ravanis, K. and Papamichael, G. (1993) Didactic destabilisation of preschool age children's spontaneous representations about the melting and vaporisation phenomena. *Pedagogical Review (Pedagogiki Epitheorisi)*, Vol. 19, pp. 308–38.

Velopoulou, A. (1998) Elements for the introduction of the concept of natural time in kindergarten. University of Aix-Marseille postgraduate paper, 2nd

Pan-Hellenic Conference of OMEP: *Postgraduate evolutions and perspectives on preschool and primary school education*, Athens, 23–24 January.

Voutsina, C. and Ravanis, K. (1998) Light as a physical entity in the thought of preschool age children: didactic approach. (University of Patras) *Researching the Children's World (Erevnondas ton kosmo tou pediou)* (scientific journal published by OMEP), Vol. 3, pp. 84–98.

Voutsina, Ch. (1998) Introducing children of preschool age to the process of questioning-speculating: an example drawn out of mathematics. University of Aix-Marseille postgraduate paper, 2nd Pan-Hellenic Conference of OMEP: *Postgraduate evolutions and perspectives on preschool and primary school education*, Athens, 23–24 January.

Zacharos, K. (1995) The contribution of social 'significance' in the comprehension of the meaning of area by preschool and early primary school children. *Contemporary Education (Synchroni Ekpedefsi)*, Vol. 81, pp. 79–84.

7. Language

Anagnostopoulos, B. D. (1995) 'Helidona's' song. *Researching the Children's World (Erevnondas ton Kosmo tou Pediou)* (scientific journal published by OMEP), Vol. 1, pp. 123–30.

Bablekou, Z. (1996) Difficulties in the development of written speech in children: characteristics–reasoning–intervention. *Researching the Children's World (Erevnondas ton Kosmo tou Pediou)* (scientific journal published by OMEP), Vol. 2, pp. 49–63.

Georgalidis, M. (1996) Pragmatic aspects of first language acquisition. Example: the formation of directives. 11th International Conference of Applied Linguistics, Proceedings, Vol. 7, Volos, Greece.

Kalabaliki-Baou, Th. (1997) Tradition-like source of language activities in kindergarten. University of Thessalia, Municipality of Iolkos: *Child and Tradition*, Volos, 11–13 April.

Kambas, A., Angelousis, N., Kioumourtjoglou, E. and Mavromatis, G. (1998) Relation between factors of psycho-kinetic development and writing-kinetic abilities in preschool age. *Researching the Children's World (Erevnondas ton kosmo tou Pediou)* (scientific journal published by OMEP), Vol. 3, pp. 57–71.

Kaplanoglou, M. (1995): Once upon a time there were lots of fairies...from folk storytelling to postwar children's literature. *Researching the Children's World (Erevnondas ton Kosmo tou Pediou)* (scientific journal published by OMEP), Vol. 1, pp. 131–9.

Kitsaras George, (1994) Reading 'preferences' of children aged $3\frac{1}{2}$ – 8 years old. *Routes (Diadromes)*, Vol. 34, pp. 158–61.

Kondoyianni, Al., (1997). Creating books with gypsy minorities' children in Greece. OMEP World Conference, Quebec, August.

Laloumis-Vidalis, E. (1996) Parents' participation in the culture of pre-reading skills of preschool age children. *Researching the Children's World (Erevnondas ton Kosmo tou Pediou)* (scientific journal published by OMEP),

Vol. 2, pp. 64–79.

Manolitsis, G. and Michalopoulou, S. with Bagiokos, G. (1996) Persuasion phenomena in children's speech: conversation analysis. *Researching the Children's World (Erevnondas ton Kosmo tou Pediou)* (scientific journal published by OMEP), Vol. 2, pp. 80–94.

Matezofski-Nikoltsou, C. M. (1995) Multi-faceted art activities that enhance and complement the development of language skills in young children. *Researching the Children's World (Erevnondas ton Kosmo tou Pediou)* (scientific journal published by OMEP), Vol. 1, pp. 140–9.

Matezofski-Nikoltsou, C. M. with Manna, A. (1995) Language events in combination with art activities for preschool children. *Ta Ekpedeftika*, Vol. 39, pp. 93–102.

Mitakidou, S. and Manna, A. (1996) Fairy-tales as a window to the world for the young child. *Researching the Children's World (Erevnondas ton Kosmo tou Pediou)* (scientific journal published by OMEP), Vol. 2, pp. 129–36.

Moschovaki, H. (1996) Teacher's story-reading styles and their impact on young children's language, attention, participation and cognitive engagement. Doctoral Dissertation, University of Bristol, presentation at the European Conference for Preschool Education, Lisbon, 1–4 September.

Papadopoulou, I. (1994) The use of children's literature in the intellectual sector of the new curriculum for kindergarten. *Diardomes (Routes)*, Vol. 34, pp. 153–7.

Stavrou, L. and Sarris, D. (1996) An application of the experimental didactic, aiming at the child's learning of written speech. University of Ioannina, Department of Preschool Education, Workshop of Special and Remedial Education and UFR de Psychologie et des Sciences de l'Education, Laboratoire EURED, Université de Toulouse-Le Mirail, France.

Stavrou, L. and Sarris, D. (1997) 'Psycho-genesis' or 'Socio-genesis' of the writing ability? University of Ioannina, Department of Preschool Education, Workshop of Special and Remedial Education and UFR de Psychologie et des Sciences de l'Education, Laboratoire EURED, Université de Toulouse-Le Mirail, France.

Stavrou, L. with Sarris, D. (1997) Writing or drawing: the child's process of learning the written speech. A psycho-socio-genetical approach. University of Ioannina, Department of Preschool Education, Workshop of Special and Remedial Education and UFR de Psychologie et des Sciences de l'Education, Laboratoire EURED, Université de Toulouse-Le Mirail, France.

Yannicopoulou, A. (1998) Parents and pre-reading. *Researching the Children's World (Erevnondas ton Kosmo tou Pediou)* (scientific journal published by OMEP), Vol. 3, pp. 11–20.

Yannikopoulou, A. (1995) What preschool children think about the heroes of fairy tales, in A. Anagnostopoulos and K. Liapis (eds.) *Folk Tales and Traditional Storytellers in Greece*. Athens: Kastaniotis.

Yiannikopoulou, A. (1995) Criteria of identification of preschoolers with the heroes of children's books. *Diadromes (Routes)*, Vol. 37, pp. 55–9.

Yiannikopoulou, A. (1995) Punishment in the world of fairy tales and what preschool children think about it. *Family and School Journal* (Cyprus), Vol. 127, pp. 18–25.

Yiannikopoulou, A. (1996) Do children of preschool and school age know and understand the main motives/themes of fairy tales?, in E. Avdikos (ed.) *From Fairy Tales to Comics*. Athens: Odysseus editions.

Yiannikopoulou, A. (1996) The animals in the Aesopic fables and the preschooler's reaction to them. *Diadromes (Routes)*, Vol. 42, pp. 90–8.

Yiannikopoulou, A. (1996) Ethical lessons from Aesopus to preschoolers. *Researching the Children's World (Erevnondas ton Kosmo tou Pediou)* (scientific journal published by OMEP), Vol. 2, pp. 119–28.

8. Arts

Aidonopoulou, E. (1998) The approach of the teaching process for children at preschool age through the music-educational system of Carl Orff. University of Exeter postgraduate paper, 2nd Pan-Hellenic Conference of OMEP: *Postgraduate evolutions and perspectives on preschool and primary school education*, Athens, 23–24 January.

Charalambous, A. (1998) Music at school. *Researching the Children's World (Erevnondas ton Kosmo tou Pediou)* (scientific journal published by OMEP), Vol. 3, pp. 219–23.

Kondoyianni, Al. (1994) Drama: exercises and techniques that preschool teachers use. Conference of Preschool Education, University of Ioannina, May.

Kondoyianni, Al. (1995) *Puppetry (Kouklotheatro)*. Monograph. Athens: Ellinika Grammata.

Kotandoula, D. (1998) The factors that influence kindergarten children in choosing the theme for 'free' drawing. *Researching the Children's World (Erevnondas ton Kosmo tou Pediou)* (scientific journal published by OMEP), Vol. 3, pp. 209–18.

Matezofski-Nikoltsou, C. M. (1994) A developmental programme of art activity procedures with young children. 2nd Conference of the Chamber of Arts: Educational Questioning on Arts, Athens, May. Published as University memorandum, *Arts: Artistic Activities for Preschool Age*. Thessalonika: University of Thessaloniki, pp. 21–38.

Matezofski-Nikoltsou, C. M. (1996) An approach to the traditional folk arts with preschool age children through a developmental arts activity programme. *Researching the Children's World (Erevnondas ton Kosmo tou Pediou)* (scientific journal published by OMEP), Vol. 2, pp. 152–60.

Matezofski-Nikoltsou, C. M. (1996) Open-face masks: an alternative solution for creative, aesthetic and safe masks. *Art Education (Eikastiki Pedia)* (published by Art Teachers Union), Vol. 12, pp. 78–82.

Sergi, Lenia (1996) Music education as a factor for the formation of the personality of the child: interdisciplinary method of teaching with music as central core, to children aged 4–6 years old. Doctoral Dissertation, University of Athens. 1st Conference of OMEP, Athens, April.

Trimi, E. (1996) A developmental art programme for preschool education based on the principles of the 'in-whole' and 'in-depth' approach. Research implementation with 'scrap paper' material. *Researching the Children's World (Erevnondas ton Kosmo tou Pediou)* (scientific journal published by OMEP), Vol. 2, pp. 137–51.

Tsarouchis, K. (1998) Teaching and learning through drama in education. University of Durham postgraduate paper, 2nd Pan-Hellenic Conference of OMEP: *Postgraduate evolutions and perspectives on preschool and primary school education*, Athens, 23–24 January.

Yiannopoulou, C. (1994) Journal of an exhibition of paintings and handicrafts in kindergarten. *Educating Community (Ekpedeftiki Kinotita)*, Vol. 28, pp. 47–50.

9. Sex education, environmental and health education, computer science and technology

(a) Sex education

Dragasi, E. (1995) Sex education for preschool and primary school age children. *Researching the Children's World (Erevnondas ton Kosmo tou Pediou)* (scientific journal published by OMEP), Vol. 1, pp. 99–106.

Kakavoulis, A. (1996) Sexual development and education. Psychological Development and Education of the Young Child. Department of Nursery School Teachers Training, University of Crete, Rethymno.

(b) Environmental and health education

Frantzi, A. (1994) Environmental education in kindergarten. *Environmental Education (Perivallontiki Ekpedefsi)*, Vol. 7, pp. 15–18.

Chrisafidis, K. (1995) Environmental education in kindergarten. *Contemporary Education (Synchroni Ekpedefsi)*, Vol. 81, pp. 71–8.

Leoditsi-Gianni, E., Pitsili, Th., Piloudi, Z., Atsi, E. and Kannakoudi, G. (1995) Eating habits of children of preschool age in today's Greece. *Contemporary Education (Synchroni Ekpedefsi)*, Vol. 80, pp. 74–8.

Tamoutseli, K. (1998) Landscapes, education and preschool age children. University of Thessaloniki Doctoral Dissertation, 2nd Pan-Hellenic Conference of OMEP: *Postgraduate evolutions and perspectives on preschool and primary school education*, Athens, 23–24 January.

(c) Computer science and technology

Doliopoulou, E. (1998) Computers in the preschool education in Greece. *Researching the Children's World (Erevnondas ton Kosmo tou Pediou)* (scientific journal published by OMEP), Vol. 3, pp. 24–34.

Doliopoulou, E. (1997) Microcomputer experience and math performance of young children. Doctoral Dissertation, Columbia University, New York, in *META-ptichiaka: ekseliksis & prooptikes stin proscholiki & protoscholiki agogi*

(*Postgraduate evolution and perspectives in preschool and primary school education*). Athens: Ellinika Grammata.

Kaila, M. and Theodoropoulou, E. (1995) An example scheme of developmental activities in kindergarten. The evolution of didactic, scientific attestation (*I ekseliksi tis didactikis, epistimologiki theorisi*). Athens: Pedagogical series, pp. 393–406.

Katsikis, A., Kossyvaki, F., Mikropoulos, A. and Savranidis, Ch. (1995) Presentation of concepts in preschool education aided by computer's interactive environment. *Researching the Children's World* (*Erevnondas ton Kosmo tou Pediou*) (scientific journal published by OMEP), Vol. 1, pp. 18–27.

Michailides, M. (1994) The use of computers by children of preschool age. *Contemporary Education* (*Synchroni Ekpedefsi*), Vol. 77, pp. 62–4.

Nikolidakis, N. (1994) Computers and language training. *School and Life* (*Scholio & Zoi*), Vol. 7–8–9, pp. 245–52.

Pange, P. (1996) Introducing computers to children in kindergarten, using multimedia applications. Aristotle University of Thessaloniki – Anniversary (under publication).

Pange, P. and Tsitouridou, M. (1995) Early childhood education on traffic policies (a multimedia application). 5th European Conference on the Quality of Early Childhood Education, Paris.

Papathanasiou, A. and Pianou, A. (1995) Specialists' aspects about the effects of video and television on children and young people. *Researching the Children's World* (*Erevnondas ton Kosmo tou Pediou*) (scientific journal published by OMEP), Vol. 1, pp. 107–20.

10. General subjects

Arapaki, X. (1994) Trial implementation of the use of markers and colours as a medium of education of children. *Free Pedagogical Step* (*Elefthero Pedagogiko Vima*), Vol. 2, pp. 3–5 and Vol. 3, pp. 3–5.

Geniataki, I., Kourti, E., Terzakis, F., Stamatopoulos, Th. and Arvanitis, S. (1995) The first days in kindergarten. Proceedings of the Scientific Congress: Psychological Development and Education of the Young Child, Crete, May.

Kaila, M. and Theodoropoulou, E. (1994) The game seen through the experience of the preschool education in Greece. *Preschool Education* (*Proscholiki Agogi*), Vol. 7–8, pp. 61–3.

Kambas, A. (1996) The development of 'rough' and 'fine' kinetic abilities. University of Thrace postgraduate paper, 2nd Pan-Hellenic Conference of OMEP: *Postgraduate evolutions and perspectives on preschool and primary school education*, Athens, 23–24 January.

Palaiologou, I. and Frouzaki, N. (1995) Are preschool children able to learn history? 5th Pan-Hellenic Seminar of Preschool Educators (TEI): Contemporary Pedagogical Approach. Thessaloniki, 25–26 November.

Petrogiannis, K. G. and Melhuish, E. C. (1994) A comparison of infants in daycare centre and home care in Greece. 13th Biennial Meeting of the

International Society for the Study of Behavioural Development, Amsterdam, 28 June–2 July.

Tsapakidou, A. (1998) Developing preschool age children's kinetic abilities via an approach of space concepts. University of Thessaloniki Doctoral Dissertation, 2nd Pan-Hellenic Conference of OMEP: *Postgraduate evolutions and perspectives on preschool and primary school education*, Athens, 23–24 January.

6

Early Educational Research in Ireland

Nóirín Hayes

Introduction

In order to understand the position of research in early education in Ireland one must understand the social and political context from which such research has emerged. For this reason it is necessary to review certain aspects of Irish life and attitudes about families, children and their education.

There are two main factors which have driven the development of early education services and the direction of research over the last 30 years in Ireland. They are the 'disadvantage' factor and the 'equality' factor. Under the heading of disadvantage there has been a growing acknowledgement that quality early educational interventions can have a positive, long-term effect on children who are at risk of educational failure. The first early intervention project in Ireland was set up in Rutland Street, Dublin in 1969 (Kellaghan, 1977; Holland, 1979). The equality lobby has been prominent in highlighting lack of childcare as a factor inhibiting women from equal access to job opportunities. This has led to a number of reports on the situation regarding childcare in Ireland, most recently the Report of the Second Commission on the Status of Women (1993) and the Report of the Working Group on Childcare Facilities for Working Parents (1994), both presenting various recommendations for improving provision and access on the ground.

These two strands have focused attention on the issue of early education from quite different perspectives – the first an education focus and the second a care focus. In as much as there has been research around early education this artificial division into care and education has, in the main, been maintained. In relation to provision and supervision of early years services the division of responsibility between the Departments of Health, on the one hand, and Education on the other remains steadfast. A recently agreed programme for government *Partnership 2000* (1996) has charged the Department of Justice, Equality and Law Reform to formulate a National Framework for the Childcare Sector. It is anticipated that this will be achieved through consultation and collaboration. To this end a multi-disciplinary, multi-agency expert Working Group was formed in July 1997. Such a modus operandi should create cohesion in a very divided sector and will, in time, improve opportunities for research. The Working Group is due to report by the end of 1998. It is interesting to note that the Minister for Education has announced his intention to host a National Early Education Convention early in 1998; how this will link with the Working Group on Childcare is, as yet, unclear.

Changes in Irish society

Irish society has undergone a radical change in the last 40 years. Up to the 1950s Ireland was a pre-industrial state with very traditional values characterised by a largely agrarian population typified by late and few marriages and large family units (Lee, 1989). Writers of this time suggest that there was a complacency among the Irish and an acceptence of the status quo. Basil Chubb (1982) writing about the pre-1960s Ireland observed that

> Few enquiries of any depth were made into social and economic problems, and even those were mostly of pedestrian quality . . . New social services and new legislation tended to follow mutatis mutandis the existing British pattern. Neither public servants (politician or professional) nor the universities provided new ideas, and there were few attempts to observe and adapt the experience of countries other than the United Kingdom. (p. 20)

The 1960s heralded a time of industrial expansion, a radical approach to the economy and new thinking in Ireland but in certain areas we continued to be slower to develop. For instance the 1908 Childcare Act was the main legislation governing the area of protection and welfare of children in Ireland until the full implementation of the Child Care Act (1991) in December 1996. Interestingly the last section of the Act to be signed into law was that covering the regulation and supervision of preschool services – the first such legislation in Ireland.

Lee (1989) identified a number of factors which marked the transition from 'Traditional Ireland' to 'Contemporary Ireland', among them our entry into the European Economic Community (EEC) in

1973. An example of the impact of this move was the response to the EEC Directive on Equal Pay which led to an Equal Pay Act in 1974. Among the provisions of this Act was the requirement for equal pay for equal work. According to Richardson (1995) its introduction only followed intense lobbying from the combined forces of the growing women's movement in Ireland. This directive was one of the first incidences of the EU requiring that the Irish legislature should treat its citizens equally.

There has been a continued increase in the number of women and mothers working outside the home in Ireland. Major changes have occurred in the workplace since the 1960s with an increase in industrialisation, part-time and seasonal work, more jobs in the service industries and less in the agriculture sector. More women are now working and more mothers are staying on in employment. Historically there has been a low participation rate of women in the labour force in Ireland. This may in part be due to the way in which Irish women have been idealised as mothers at the expense of opportunities for employment. The ideology of motherhood is reinforced by our Constitution (1937) which makes special reference to the position of the family, women and children. Article 41.2.1. identifies the special position of women in the home:

> In particular the State recognises that by her life within the home woman gives to the State a support without which the common good cannot be achieved.

Article 41.2.2., with particular reference to the mother, states that

> The State shall, therefore, endeavour to ensure that mothers shall not be obliged by economic necessity to engage in labour to the neglect of their duties in the home.

The recent report of the Constitution Review Group (1996a) states that 'Article 41.2 assigns to women a domestic role as wives and mothers. It is a dated provision much criticised in recent years. Notwithstanding its terms, it has not been of any particular assistance even to women working exclusively within the home' (p. 333).

In terms of impact on women and children our entry into the EEC coincided with a rise in the women's movement and a questioning of the prescribed, domestic role of Irish women. It was not until the early 1970s, for instance, that the marriage bar, imposed in 1929, was lifted. This bar required female civil servants and local authority workers to resign on marriage. Coupled with the Constitution the marriage bar made a very clear statement about the role of women and mothers.

It is fair to conclude that the change in participation rates of married women and mothers in the labour force – and the related need for childcare – was speeded up by the removal of the marriage bar and the introduction of equal pay legislation.

Richardson (1995) reports participation rates for women in the workforce as having changed from 29 per cent in 1961 to 39 per cent in 1996 (Labour Force Survey Reports 1961–96). More dramatic is the rate of change of the participation rate of married women from 7.5 per cent in 1971 to 31.3 per cent in 1993. The percentage of women with children in the workforce was 39.8 in 1993 with 25 per cent of mothers whose youngest child is 3–9 years in employment. It is clear that there are an increasing number of women in Ireland who are combining employment outside the home and the care of young children along with their domestic and housekeeping duties.

Associated with the changes outlined above is an equally dramatic change in marriage rates – 7.1 per 1,000 population in 1970 to 4.4 per 1,000 in 1993; birth rates – 74,000 in 1980 down to 49,000 in 1993; and family size – the average family size has dropped from 3.23 in 1980 to 1.93 in 1993 (Commission on the Family, 1996). The number of separated persons rose from 37,245 in 1986 to 55,143 in 1991 and Millar, Leeper and Davies (1992) found that 10 per cent of all families with children under 15 years of age were lone-parent families and only 25 per cent of these families received an income from employment. All of these changes and trends have implications for the delivery of early years services and, one might expect, a rise in interest in researching this area of provision.

There is no doubt that Ireland is experiencing an economic boom at the moment and this is characterised in the media by reference to Ireland as the Celtic Tiger. However, despite increased employment opportunities and more jobs being created, unemployment, particularly long-term unemployment and the risk of poverty it brings for families with children, continues to pose a major challenge to society and policy-makers. In 1994 the level of child poverty was estimated as a 29 per cent risk for children compared to an 18 per cent risk for adults at the 50 per cent poverty line (Callan *et al.*, 1996).

Poverty, educational disadvantage and early education

There appears to be a close link between poverty and educational disadvantage. In a study on the impact of poverty in Ireland Whelan (1994) found that:

- 25 per cent of those with no educational qualifications live in poverty

- 4 per cent of those with a Leaving Certificate or better live in poverty

- 3 out of 4 poor households are headed by a person with no educational qualifications

- 60 per cent of those who were unemployed for more than a year have no educational qualifications.

The statistics above paint a clear picture but the relationship between poverty and education is complex and the interaction of a wide variety of factors contribute to individual cases. Attention to the issue of poverty in Ireland and particularly the role that education might play in overcoming poverty, has increased with our overall prosperity and generated recommendations regarding early childhood services and some evaluative research of different initiatives.

The previous government, following extensive collaboration, implemented a National Anti Poverty Strategy (NAPS). The challenge of tackling poverty and social exclusion was identified as requiring a strategic approach involving all government departments. The report highlighted education as having an important role in the promotion of equality of opportunity and educational intervention and recommended that support must begin at the earliest stage of education. 'The report, under Policy Action, identifies increasing preschool services as one important strategy' (Hayes, 1997). As an Objective One area in the EU, Ireland has attracted a high level of funding supporting initiatives to improve the quality of life for those currently living in poverty, including support for the development of community-based childcare services.

In line with the recognition that education has an important role in breaking the cycle of disadvantage, the Department of Education has aimed at 'Breaking the Cycle' (Kellaghan *et al.*, 1996). Among the strategies outlined is the development of a headstart type preschool initiative called the Early Start. This initiative, launched in 1994, is preventative rather than remedial in nature and recognises that school failure is a social as well as an educational problem. The Department of Education White Paper *Charting our Education Future* (1995) presents a framework for the future development of Irish education which takes account of the rapidly changing and evolving society. The rationale for developing preschooling under the Department of Education is that such educational intervention, in cases where children are at risk of educational failure, may counteract later school failure. This belief is based on three principles:

- Early childhood experiences are important for the child's development.

- Entry to formal schooling is a major transition for children, particularly those having a disadvantaged background.

- Early disadvantages affect the child's enduring experience within formal schooling, since such disadvantages tend to be both persistent and cumulative.

The overall aim of the Early Start intervention programme is to *compensate* (italics added) for background deprivation and in this way support the optimum development of the child (Ireland, 1995, pp, 15–17). The Early Start centres provide an educational intervention for 3–4-year-olds in designated disadvantaged areas. They provide a 2 1/2-hour programme for children which emphasises language and cognitive development. Each centre is staffed by a primary school teacher and a childcare assistant.

The research informing the development of an early educational intervention such as the Early Start is largely international as the only Irish study that has evaluated the longitudinal impact of early education is the Rutland Street project. This compensatory preschool project was supported by the Department of Education and the Van Leer Foundation. It opened in 1969 and ran as a research project until 1974. The preschool service itself is still running and is under the control of the Department of Education. The Rutland Street project was evaluated under the direction of the Department of Education through their research centre – the Education Research Centre – in Dublin. This centre has also been commissioned to evaluate the impact of the first eight Early Start centres and is due to report by the end of 1997. Results of the effectiveness of the Rutland Street project for the children attending were in line with other projects of the time and showed that the gains in the children's scholastic performance had not been maintained beyond early junior school (Kellaghan, 1977; Holland, 1979). A follow-up study of the children at age sixteen, however, found that participants were more likely to remain on in school and take public examinations than the control group (Kellaghan and Greaney, 1993). The Department's reliance on the Rutland Street project as a model preschool provision is evidenced by the fact that the curriculum guidelines given to the primary teachers in September 1994 in preparation for running the Early Start programme were the same guidelines prepared for the Rutland Street teachers in 1969.

The main responsibility of the Department of Education is, however, to first, second and third level education and their role in preschool provision is only seen in terms of intervention projects to counteract the risk of later school failure among disadvantaged children. Despite a compulsory school starting age of six years, the majority of Irish four-year-olds and all five year olds enter the primary school system through the junior and senior infant classes. The Department noted in the White Paper (Ireland, 1995) that the role of the infant classes is such that much of what is considered preschooling in many other countries is already incorporated in the Irish primary school system for children between four and six. This claim has been disputed by the Irish National Teachers Organisation (INTO) and a number of academics who argue that the training of teachers, the structure of the classes, the class sizes, the curriculum and the lack of inservice support to infant teachers make delivery of an appropriate early years curriculum within the primary system very difficult (INTO, 1995; Hayes, 1994). A recent study has confirmed the academic nature of infant classes where observations show that more time is spent in the classroom on pre-academic activities than any other activity and more teacher time is spent in didactic teaching than in any other behaviour (Hayes, O'Flaherty with Kernan, 1997).

There has been an explosion of growth in the early years service sector since the 1980s. While many of the developments were in response to the needs of working parents there was also a general sense that quality early years experiences were valuable to children in and of themselves. Accurate figures regarding the number and type of services in what might be called the informal, unregulated early years sector are very hard to come by. Despite the growth in services there has been very little research carried out into the types of early services emerging or the effects of early educational experiences on children and families in Ireland. What research has been carried out has tended to be at postgraduate level and rarely published. In a listing of research in early education in Ireland, including research in the junior and senior infant classes of primary schools, there were eighty papers, MA and PhD theses noted (UCC, 1997). When studied further it transpires that only five entries, all papers, have been published. Seventy of the listings were written within the last twenty years and four of the remaining ten listings were 1970 Masters theses associated with the Rutland Street project. Furthermore twenty-nine of the listings refer to postgraduate studies awarded in the North of Ireland which focus, in the main, on the British educational system, a system that is quite different from that in Ireland. What is most noteworthy is the enormous rise in research in early education that has occurred since 1990.

It is the lack of data about what provision is available, who is using it and what level of quality exists that has fuelled much of the recent research in early education. The Commission on the Family, established in 1995 by the Minister for Social Welfare, was charged to 'examine the needs and priorities of families in a rapidly changing social and economic environment' (*Commission on the Family*, Ireland, 1996, p. 8). In pursuit of this aim the Commission sought submissions from the public. Thirty-six per cent of the total submissions received were concerned with childcare (third highest category, with education and counselling at first and second place respectively) and, in response, the Commission requested the Economic and Social Research Institute (ESRI) to carry out a national survey of childcare use in conjunction with its monthly consumer survey. The ESRI agreed and carried out the survey over a three-month period. Results of this first national survey of parents regarding their use of childcare will be published in early 1998.

The voluntary or non-governmantal sector has been so poorly resourced that it has been as much as it could do to register and advise members on issues around providing a quality service. There has been no research published under the Irish Preschool Playgroups Association (IPPA) or the National Children's Nursery Association (NCNA) although the former has recently secured EU funds to carry out two cross-border studies (a) into rural daycare needs and (b) into the introduction of the HighScope programme in selected preschool playgroups. In addition both the above associations have been willing to allow their members (where members have agreed) to act as subjects for small-scale research projects which postgraduate students may be undertaking.

The organisation supporting the Irish-medium playgroups, An Comhchóiste Réamhscolaíochta Teo., have through the Irish Language Institute had input to a number of research projects around early education and second language acquisition. One factor which has allowed this research to take place is that, given the central position of the Irish language in Ireland, there is preferential access to funding which is available because of the Irish language focus of the research. This is not so readily available to others researching early education. The most recent publication by Hickey (1997) gives a very clear introduction to readers of the experiences of children, families and early years workers who choose to work through the medium of Irish. The growth of the naíonraí, or Irish-medium playschools, has raised many educational and psychological questions that are addressed in this large-scale study. Data were gathered from those directly involved in the naíonraí – parents, providers, advisers and children. The study shows that children make significant advances in the Irish language during their period in the naíonraí which leads to increased use of Irish in their homes as well. The report contains many recommendations for the future development of this form of early childhood service and has important messages for policy-makers in relation to both Irish language teaching and early education in its broadest sense.

The childcare agency Barnardos was one of the first voluntary services to commission research into its own early years services. The result was a book, *Intervention in the Early Years* (O'Flaherty, 1995), which evaluated the implementation of the HighScope curriculum in a Barnardos nursery. This review is similar to one supported by the Dublin Institute of Technology which evaluated a community-based preschool service in Dublin's inner city (O'Flaherty *et al.*, 1994). Both studies identify the need for more of the longitudinal research necessary to evaluate the long-term impact of such programmes but recognise the difficulty in accessing funding for such studies. Barnardos itself has been commissioned to carry out work by different groups, including the Department of Health, around local policy on early service provision and support.

EU funds for disadvantaged areas and equality of opportunity initiatives have occasionally included funding for, inter alia, the development of childcare services. One of the prerequisites for accessing these funds is that projects supported would be evaluated and in this way we have the promise of an increased store of data around childcare/early education. It is worth noting that the evaluations carried out are around equality issues or disadvantage rather than focusing on the children and the impact of the services on children. Some of the studies do, however, refer specifically to aspects of the projects which are relevant to how such services impact on the child and family. Not all these reports could be considered as research but there are some exceptions. In a recent initiative the Department of Justice, Equality and Law Reform allocated money to local childcare initiatives under the direction of the Area Development Management Ltd. (ADM). ADM was established in 1994 and acts as an intermediary company to support local social and economic development. As part of their responsibility in the Childcare Initiative, launched in 1994, they commissioned an independent social researcher to evaluate the effectiveness of the project. The report by McKeown and Fitzgerald was published in 1997 and represents an important first step in a close look at how we provide at community level for our very young children, and particularly those who are from families that are economically and/or socially disadvantaged. Although his terms of reference were to evaluate the value for money of the investment – which was for capital childcare costs only – McKeown widened his brief to look at such issues as staff–child ratio, costs and equipment, and presented, for the first time, a picture of service provision on the ground. As with all good research this work acts as a taster for future research. ADM has also commissioned smaller policy-related research around the provision of full-day childcare in areas of disadvantage and the results of these studies are eagerly awaited.

Also coming under the broad heading of research, funded through the equality line of EU funds, are a number of projects which focused on childcare. They have been funded through the New Opportunity for Women strand. These projects have been, by the nature of the funding requirements, development rather than research oriented but, given the impoverished nature of the information we have about childcare, they act as a source of interesting data (Department of Enterprise and Employment, 1994). In the 1995–97 round of funding there were four such projects funded in Ireland. Two of the projects developed a community-based childcare service under the direction of local committees. Both projects required market research around local need before development began and this material will give some idea of what the demand for childcare is in the communities covered. A third project developed a mobile training and support service in early education in a rural area and the final childcare project aimed to develop a national framework for childcare training using, where appropriate, Accreditation of Prior Learning (APL). This latter project was under the direction of the Early Childhood Research Centre at the Dublin Institute of Technology. Reports from these studies and their overall evaluation will be available in early 1998.

The educationally focused research into early childhood services has tended to be small scale and the national studies have focused in the main on surveying teachers about the implementation of curriculum in school settings. The most recent survey of relevance to our topic was carried out in 1995 by the INTO and involved a survey of junior infant teachers – that is, primary teachers who are teaching four- and five-year-olds. Such teachers follow the national curriculum known as the New Curriculum (1971). Results are reported in *Early Childhood Education: Issues and Concerns* (INTO, 1995). As this is a study of teachers by their union it is no surprise to find that a great deal of the information sought and received was around issues of conditions of service and structural issues such as class sizes and available equipment and resources. Nonetheless the final report contains a wide-ranging overview of this aspect of early education in Ireland and the survey results do touch on issues of importance to the type and quality of the early education provided for children of this age. It too raises questions for future research. For instance, one area surveyed was that of teaching style and results indicate that:

- 65 per cent of teachers surveyed frequently used whole-class instruction

- 55 per cent frequently used formal group teaching (with grouping based on ability)

- 51 per cent frequently used informal group teaching

- 60 per cent frequently used teacher-directed individual activities

- 41 per cent frequently used child-directed individual activities.

When asked to indicate preferred teaching styles the percentages alter in the expected direction with 71 per cent indicating child-directed individual activities. (It is interesting to note that similar results were found in a study carried out by O'Rourke and Archer in 1987.) In commenting on the above results the report's author writes 'Teachers recognise that the conditions which pertain in their classroom are not ideal and change their teaching style accordingly' (p. 130). Style of interaction between adult and child is so crucial a factor in quality early education that this is an area needing further research.

The weaknesses of the survey method are well known and acknowledged by those who use it but the time and cost constraints of observational research can be prohibitive. In 1994 private funding – augmented with funding from the Department of Education and the Combat Poverty Agency – was secured by the Early Childhood Research Centre in the Dublin Institute of Technology to participate in the IEA Preprimary Project. This study is a carefully designed comparative study of the experiences of four-year-olds in different early years settings. The primary aim of the Irish element of the study was to describe the quality of early years experiences of a sample of 400 Irish four-year-olds in 100 different settings – 50 in designated disadvantaged settings. As a nationally representative observational study this marks an important development in early years research in Ireland. The findings – reported in *A Window on Early Education in Ireland* (Hayes, O'Flaherty with Kernan, 1997) – raise a number of issues for consideration in relation to practice, provision, policy and research. The study provides empirical data which confirms the findings of the INTO study (above) that whole-class instruction is the most common teaching style in our junior infant classes.

It is intended that the report of this study will generate discussion, debate and action which will lead to improvements in the availability and quality of services for young children. The next phase of the project – a study of the same sample of children at age seven – has just commenced. In addition two postgraduate students are using the data as the research base for their theses.

Conclusion

Because early years service provision in Ireland is so varied and only now becoming regulated, much of the research in the field has been descriptive, evaluative and applied in nature. It has been carried out as commissioned research by academics or research consultants and used to direct or initiate policy on early services for young children. Funding comes from varied but limited sources including government departments.

There has been a remarkable rise in the attention given to early years services since the beginning of the 1990s and this is reflected in the growing number of published articles and reports and the vibrant postgraduate research base that is emerging in the major third-level institutions. These more recent research projects have a wider, more academic focus than earlier work.

As yet there is no well-established early years forum for discussion and debate; neither is there any national journal focusing on early years in Ireland. However, with the growth of interest in early childhood and an increase in research studies it is hoped that such developments will follow. Indeed, as evidence of a growing interest in the area, a recent meeting of the Psychological Society of Ireland hosted a well-attended symposium on Issues in Early Childhood Service Provision with speakers from Ireland, the UK and the USA. In addition, two third-level institutions, University College Cork and the Dublin Institute of Technology, have secured funding for research centres with a particular focus on early childhood studies. It is anticipated that the next few years will see a more vibrant and co-ordinated approach to early years research with increased opportunities for sharing information and widening the impact of research on policy, provision and practice.

References

Bunreacht na h Éireann (Constitution of Ireland) (1937). Dublin: Stationery Office.

Callan, T. Nolan, B., Whelan, B., Whelan, C. and Williams, J. (1996) *Poverty in the 1990s.* The Economic and Social Research Institute and Combat Poverty Agency, Dublin. Oaktree Press.

Chubb, B. (1982) *The Government and Politics of Ireland.* London: Langman.

Department of Education (1971) *Handbook for Teachers Vols. 1 and 2.* Dublin: Stationery Office, Government Publications.

Department of Enterprise and Employment (1994) *Making their Mark: The Experiences of Childcare Projects within the NOW Programmes in Ireland.* Dublin: Stationery Office/Council of Status of Women.

Hayes, N. (1995) *The Case for a National Policy on Early Education.* Combat Poverty Agency Discussion Paper No. 2. Dublin: Combat Poverty Agency.

Hayes, N. (1997) Social exclusion and Irish policy regarding early interventions. Paper presented at the 28th Psychological Society of Ireland Conference, Ennis, November.

Hayes, N., O'Flaherty, J. with Kernan, M. (1997) *A Window on Early Education in Ireland.* Dublin: Dublin Institute of Technology.

Hennessy, E. and Hayes, N. (1997) Early childhood services in Ireland. *International Journal of Early Years Education,* Vol 5, no. 3, pp. 211–24

Hickey, T. (1997) *Early Immersion Education in Ireland: Na Naíonraí.* Dublin: Institiœid Teangeola'ochta Éireann.

Holland, S. (1979) *Rutland Street.* Oxford: Pergamon Press and Van Leer Foundation.

INTO (Irish National Teachers Organisation) (1995) *Early Childhood Education: Issues and Concerns.* Dublin: INTO.

Ireland (1991) *Child Care Act.* Dublin: Stationery Office, Government Publications.

Ireland (1993) *Report of the Second Commission on the Status of Women.* Dublin: Stationery Office, Government Publications.

Ireland (1994) *Report of the Working Group on Childcare Facilities for Working Parents.* Dublin: Stationery Office, Government Publications.

Ireland (1995) *Charting our Educational Future, White Paper on Education.* Dublin: Stationery Office, Government Publications.

Ireland (1996) *Commission on the Family – Interim Report.* Dublin: Stationery Office, Government Publications.

Ireland (1996) *Report of the Constitution Review Group.* Dublin: Stationery Office, Government Publications.

Ireland (1996) *Partnership 2000 for Inclusion, Employment and Competitiveness.* Dublin: Stationery Office, Government Publications.

Ireland (1997) *National Anti-Poverty Strategy – Sharing the Progress.* Dublin: Stationery Office, Government Publications.

Kellaghan, T. (1977) *The Evaluation of an Intervention Programme for Disadvantaged Children.* Windsor, Berks: NFER.

Kellaghan, T. and Greaney, B. J. (1993) *The Educational Developmentof Students Following Participation in a Preschool Programme in a Disadvantaged Area.* Dublin: Educational Research Centre.

Kellaghan, T., Weir, S., Ó'hUallacháin, S. and Morgan, M. (1995) *Educational Disadvantage in Ireland.* Dublin: Department of Education, Combat Poverty Agency and the Educational Research Centre.

Lee, J. (1989) *Ireland 1912–1985, Politics and Society.* Cambridge University Press.

McKeown, K. and Fitzgerald, G. (1997) *Developing Childcare Services in Disadvantaged Areas.* Dublin: ADM.

Miller, J., Leeper, S. and Davies, C. (1992) *Lone Parents: Poverty and Public Policy in Ireland.* Dublin: Combat Poverty Agency.

O'Flaherty, J. (1995) *Intervention in the Early Years.* London: National Children's Bureau.

O'Flaherty, J., Fitzpatrick, A., Hayes, N. and McCarthy, B. (1994) *Evaluation of St Audeon's Parent Preschool Health Promotion Project.* Dublin: Dublin Institute of Technology.

O'Rourke, B. and Archer, P. (1987) A survey of teaching practice in infant classrooms in Irish primary schools. *Irish Journal of Education,* Vol. 27, pp. 53–79.

Richardson, V. (1995) Reconcliation of family life and working life, in I. Colgan McCarthy (ed.) *Irish Family Studies: Selected Papers.* Dublin: Family Study Centre, UCD.

UCC (1997) *Irish Research in Early Years Education.* Cork: Department of Education, University College Cork.

Whelan, C. T. (ed.) (1994) *Values and Social Change in Ireland.* Dublin: Gill and Macmillan.

7

Young Children Learning: Research in Poland

Malgorzata Karwowska-Struczyk

It is pleasing to contribute to a publication about early childhood education research, collaborating with Western European colleagues, firstly because I hope my chapter will contribute to the extension of knowledge about this topic among readers in Western Europe. Secondly, I have the honour of representing the one country included here which is not yet a member of the European Union. I therefore feel especially distinguished and obliged to fulfil the task I have undertaken in a proper and reliable way! I would like this book to be accessible in Polish. Such studies are not currently available in Poland, which is a pity because they could enrich theoretical and methodological experiences of the society of researchers, teachers and educational decision-makers.

The structure of this survey of early childhood education research in Poland will comprise four principal parts:

- An outline of the socio-political and economic background of Poland in the process of violent systemic, economic and ethical transformations.

- A presentation of the state of care and education for children in the preschool age in connection with macrosystem changes.

- An analysis of the results of the survey of the problems, issues and methodology of the research carried out in several academic centres and discussion of these in relation to cultural and economic conditions.[1]

---

[1] The survey contained questions concerning the problems of methodology, research paradigms, financing and implementing research results in practice, and was based on suggestions made by the editor of this book. Of 20 questionnaires sent out only 6 academic centres replied. This may have been because of lack of time, lack of

- A more detailed presentation of selected problems from the chosen research (carried out in the period 1987–1997), discussing the main research trends. This section will also include an overview of studies on the quality of experience of the children who are four years old in preschool institutions in Poland, carried out with the collaboration of 15 countries from all over the world and co-ordinated by IEA (the International Association for the Evaluation of Educational Achievements) and High/Scope Educational Foundation (USA).

Two principal sources of information were used in the study: the opinions of others on the subject (from the results of a survey and from publications) and my own experience as the participant in two communities, on one hand as a researcher and tutor, and on the other hand as a 'client' using education services.

The chapter is written from two perspectives: a kind of biographical report of my life in a definite culture in a given place will be interwoven with more scientific considerations (Bruner, 1990).

The socio-economic background

Poland is a country which, after forty years of communist regime, has started creating the mechanisms for democratic and lawful systems, both in political and in social life. The Republic of Poland has been a parliamentary democracy since 1992. The structural transformations began after 1989, as a result of the victory of social and political forces connected with Solidarity and the resolution of the so-called round table meeting of the members of the Communist Party, who had governed Poland for 45 years. This meeting brought together those who had governed since the end of the Second World War and the representatives of the democratic opposition coming from the Solidarity movement.

Only in 1992 did free democratic general elections take place in Poland, for the first time since the Second World War. These occurred at both national and local levels. Poland is a country aiming at a free market economy ruled by competition, supply and demand. At the beginning of the transformations the shift to a market economy had a severe impact on the quality of people's lives. Among these unfavourable changes one should mention:

interest in the subject, insufficient extra pay for the work done, etc. The survey was carried out in the autumn of 1996, so its results are valid as a random sample of the representatives of some research communities, who wanted to participate in the research.

- Household incomes declined by 27 per cent by the end of 1991 and this has not changed for the better in the meantime. The World Bank estimates that 5.5 million people in Poland live on the verge of poverty, mainly because of low incomes (among approximately 65 per cent of this group of the population) and unemployment (the remaining 35 per cent).

- The inflation rate rose by 250 per cent in 1989. At the moment of writing this article it has fallen to 15–17 per cent.

- The unemployment rate amounted to 14.9 per cent by 1993 (this represents 2.6 million unemployed). However, the rate has been systematically reduced to 11.6 per cent in 1997.

- The proportion of families living in poverty increased from 6 per cent in 1989 to 21 per cent in 1991 and this percentage has persisted and may even be steadily increasing.

- Many large companies are still administered by the State and sponsored by public money. The government is in a quandary about how to privatise, or reprivatise, them. Money for other State duties to society (health care, education, social welfare, security) has been spent to keep the reducing services running.

- The agriculture policy is not promoting changes and the much-needed modernisation of the old, one might say almost 'medieval', structure of this sector of the economy.

Despite the fact that there are many advantages to some of the transformations, these are not appreciated by some people and thus they do not engage with them because of their conviction that people lack self-sufficiency. This conviction is deeply rooted in the Polish culture. Present changes allowing independence (self-dependence), making one's own decisions and taking responsibility for one's own life are seen as difficult. A lot of psychologists and sociologists state that a learned hopelessness is a national feature. They claim that attitudes towards the authorities have developed as a consequence of the totalitarian system. But many in society have learnt how to use the new legal possibilities in the democratic system for self-development and the improvement of their standards of living.

Here are some of the important, positive changes:

- parliamentary democracy at national and municipal levels

- decentralisation in some sectors of the economy and social life (although the present coalition consisting of the Social Democratic

Party (SLD) and the Agricultural Party (PSL), the roots of which are in the former Communist Party and its satellites, distinctly slows down the processes).[2]

A lot of economic, political and social decisions could be taken and results achieved by the local authorities in a given territory provided the latter had the right to make the decisions and the necessary financial means at their disposal.

An example of the ineffectiveness of the State and its excessive centralisation is found in the attitude of the government during the floods, which affected the south-west regions of Poland in the summer of 1997. Representatives of opposition parties proved the government not only to be incompetent but also to have reacted insensitively to the tragedy of so many thousands of people.

Decentralisation is exemplified, for example, in the increasing number of social and private economic initiatives, emerging companies, educational institutions, banks, shops, access by foreign capital and businesses. Other aspects signalling this change include the elimination of official censorship (it is not possible to exclude the presence of autocensorship, which grows out of the residual fear established in the previous periods) and living according to one's own system of values with external freedom creating possibilities for internal freedom.

In 1996 the population of Poland was 38,580,600 of which around 62 per cent lived in towns and 38 per cent in rural areas. Around 2,130,600 (5.5 per cent) of this population represents children of preschool age (3–7 years). This group had been decreasing; for example, in 1980 it was 2,504,100; in 1994, 2,201,900. However, the number of children of preschool age has been increasing again since 1995.

Early childhood care and education provision

Early childhood provision for 3–6-year-old children is guaranteed by education law. However, the integration of preschool education into the formal system has never been reflected in relevant legal regulations or in the amount of State expenditure for this particular stage of education. The public preschool is an independent educational and teaching institution for children from 3 to 7 years of age.

A child of 6 is entitled to one year preschool preparation before entering primary school at the age of 7. This preparation consists of

---

[2] The chapter is being written before the parliamentary elections of September 1997. Change in the ruling parties is expected by many Poles.

stimulating the child's general development and teaching the primary reading skills and basic mathematics. Almost every 6-year-old attends so-called kindergarten, on a part-time basis (no more than five hours a day during a year), or preschool, which operates full-time (from five to eight or nine hours a day and children can attend for four years). Each child is expected to attend at least one year of such preparation, and it is perceived as a duty by the parents to have their children do so, although in fact this does not always happen.

The communes (local authorities) have a duty to organise kindergartens, if parents have expressed a wish for their children to attend. Though children between 3 and 6 are entitled to educational provision, access to public or private preschools and kindergartens is possible for less than 50 per cent of all children of preschool age in Poland. Only 984,545 children in this age group actually attend some kind of preschool or kindergarten. The 6-year-olds form the majority in this number (537,000, i.e. 55.6 per cent). The kindergartens are attached and related to a primary school, in terms of organisation. The setting up and running of kindergartens is commissioned by the school and financed by the commune.

Preschools and kindergartens are financed from local government's own revenues, from different sources (taxes); preschools' own incomes (such as donations, parents' fees, etc.) and the general subsidy received by the commune from the State budget. Starting from September 1990, preschools and kindergartens have been obliged to offer free places for at least five hours a day – the time necessary for the implementation of the 'Minimum Curriculum of Preschool Education'. The minimum curriculum covers the basic aims, tasks and content of preschool education for children 3–6 years of age. In the course of this work, a teacher should:

- see to the children's health and safety

- support the children's cognitive activity, providing opportunities for experiencing and recognising their own, socio-cultural and natural environments

- initiate the children's sense of identity and responsibility for their own conduct

- provide appropriate conditions for the development of the children's abilities

- ensure attention is paid to the learning requirements of children with special educational needs.

The decentralisation of preschool management and differentiated management of subjects has given rise to developments which have had a negative effect. For example, there has been a rise in tuition fees paid by parents, with a resulting reduction in demand for early childhood care and education even by employed parents. In many cases, however, it has resulted in the involvement of parents in the preschools in different ways, integrating the preschool or kindergarten with the community. From the point of view of continuity and ensuring the complementarity of the two milieus (home and preschool), the effect of this on the children's socialisation has been a very favourable phenomenon. It has also been advantageous in that knowledge about individual children has been deepened and the education strategies of the kindergarten and the home, the two most important environments in the life of the child, have been brought closer together. As Wood (1990) indicates, by engaging the local community, improvements in the development of conditions for children occur.

The phenomenon of local community mobilisation is founded on the notion that not only children make use of the programmes promoting their development, but the grown ups also engage in the programme and this produces a 'double generational effect'. First, there is an impact which causes an improvement in the quality of provision for the child but there is also a powerful influence on the adults, who, as a result of their involvement, acquire a sense of their own value and greater satisfaction from the fulfilment of their parental role, as well as being able to transfer their newly acquired abilities within the adult sphere (Wood, 1990).

However, there is a problem relating to unemployed families, who are now unable to send their children to educational settings. The nursery school for children who are three to six years old is perceived by parents as a 'childcare' institution rather than an educational one, while kindergartens, being didactic, are seen as educational. Parents and teachers understand it is the task of the kindergarten to prepare the child to meet the demands of school.

. Another factor is the unequal access to this kind of service in different regions of Poland. Historically, kindergartens were perceived as the institutions providing care and education for those children whose parents worked. At present there are larger numbers of institutions in industrialised areas compared with rural regions. Farmers have never been perceived as working class. At present, the number of children attending kindergartens in the urban areas of Upper Silesia and Warsaw is ten times higher than in the agricultural regions such as Chelm and Lomza. When the working class and the Communist

Party formed the most powerful national group, the differential was even greater. It is impossible to say exactly what caused such a situation, perhaps a mix of a lack of need for such services as well as ideological considerations. In my opinion the second was decisive. The Communists prioritised the problems of the working class that supported them.

Since preschool education is not obligatory, parents have no legal instruments they can refer to, but in the case of basic (primary) education, laws have been passed by the Polish Parliament establishing this right (Educational Act, the Constitution of the Republic of Poland). It is even possible to evoke international law, for example the United Nations Convention on the Rights of the Child, ratified by Poland. However, as yet, parents' organisations have not been developed, as in western countries. Thus they have little influence on the authorities, in seeking to improve the conditions of life and development for children.

Neither parents nor education authorities openly express any convictions about the importance of high quality experiences during early childhood as a foundation for the later stages of school and adult life. Parents have no influence upon the local and central authorities and they do not demand or achieve an entitlement to good quality care and education institutions for their young children. Neither Parliament nor the government is interested in enlarging the budgets for education. The present Polish government and the majority of those elected to Parliament represent two similar political groups. The opposition is very weak. Unfortunately this has created a situation where social need is neglected.

Meanwhile, teachers, academics and members of the research community involved in different political and theoretical aspects of the development and education of a small child disagree with this inaction. They are all convinced by evidence concerning the importance of the earliest years and their relationship to educational, social and economic success in adulthood, although a lot of them, perhaps, do not acknowledge the many faults and weaknesses of the kindergarten system, which are unfavourable for a child.

A number of factors demonstrate the lack of interest in and, in consequence, the low quality of educational services rendered by kindergartens. They include the following:

- Funding for kindergartens is not 'ring-fenced'.

- There is no central system or policy for inservice training for teachers.

- There is a lack of interest in using research evidence to inform policy and practice.

- There is no system for commissioning and financing research on early childhood education.[3] In particular, this area is not of special interest, either socially or politically, and it is very difficult for research proposals in this field to win an allocation of financial support in funding competitions.

- Low prestige of a teacher's job.

The status of early years teachers, their pay and conditions are far less favourable than for those working in primary schools. Even the teacher–pupil ratio is higher, so that meaningful interactions between teacher and child and sensitivity to individual needs are practically impossible.

Summing up, it could be said that decision-makers show little interest in improving the functioning of preschool institutions. Parents are generally satisfied with the kindergartens attended by their children. In fact, they do not appear to be interested in what is going on in their own child's kindergarten. The survey carried out as part of the research project 'European Families in the 1990s' reveals that the parents have very little contact with the kindergartens, but they claim the kindergarten is to blame for a lack of openness to local community. The survey indicates, however, that the perception of the function of the kindergarten has been changing, from one of care to that of education.[4] This fact is connected with the change of the remit of kindergartens, since they ceased providing services only for working parents. Everybody who recognises the positive value of attending such a setting, for the child, and who is able to cover the fees can make use of their services. There are no lists of parents waiting for vacancies in the kindergartens. In the former socio-political situation when this sector was not financed properly, accessibility to kindergartens was limited, and places were mainly for the children of working parents, single mothers or teachers. This provision was used by the former regime as a mechanism for social engineering, creating one favoured class.

The truth about the relation between the teacher and the child in the kindergarten is understood by academics who have access to this aspect

---

[3] In the former political conditions there was a mechanism for ordering and financing research by the Ministry of National Education into so-called key problems. Using this financing mechanism a lot of remarkable research for kindergarten education was carried out, e.g. Miller.

[4] Research project co-ordinated by Goran Lassbo from the University of Gothenburg, 'European Families in the 1990s'.

of pedagogical reality. While attending classes in the kindergarten with my preschool education students I often experience ethical conflict. My task is to make them aware of how to relate to and teach the children. What my students see in the kindergarten and what is often discussed later in seminars and tutorials should not happen. The teachers are functionaries, the executors of defined, organisational curriculum tasks and not authors of change. They are not being expected to create situations for new, innovative, practical solutions through which to respond better to children's needs and interests. Barbara Wilgocka-Okoñ (1989) emphasised this fact. In spite of changes of governing parties, it is unfortunately the case that the situation of the Polish teacher has not improved since then, even though legal regulations have been implemented allowing greater autonomy, creativity and independence.

Where is the difficulty, what mechanisms and strategies should be set in motion to change this situation? What kind of initial teacher education should be developed?

One consequence of the attitude to the young child is the attitude to early years teachers. One of those surveyed for this chapter stated: 'a child and an adult should contribute equally to interactions. But the child is still perceived as an object, subdued by the process of education.' Education is treated as the business of adults only. The contents should be prepared by an adult in such a way that they can be easily absorbed by the child. The adult conveys the content, keeps discipline, carries out a lot of routine activities (administration) but does not get involved in the real learning needs of the children. These facts are the results of the survey I will discuss later.

Research concerning the quality of experiences of children in kindergarten shows that there is a very weak correlation between the educational approaches (for example, the kinds of activities offered, the teacher's behaviour, the teacher's characteristics such as age, years of experience, etc.) and the children's achievements. These correlate much more strongly with parental level of education, their aspirations concerning their child's education, and realistic expectations concerning the child's future educational career.

What makes a difference is clearly the educational strategies used by the parents, their ways of communicating with their child, the interpretation of reality and the cultural context and value system in which they are raising their child. We can surmise that parents with higher education are more likely to value the cultural capital transmitted by the education system than parents with lower educational attainment (Janion, 1996).

On the basis of the results of research conducted with a representative sample of rural and municipal kindergartens, it is possible to make the following generalisations: what the teacher in the kindergarten performs and what the child in the kindergarten performs does not influence the child's early (four-year-old) or later (seven-year-old) development (Janion, 1996).

Such a generalisation will seem unjust to the many teachers, headteachers of kindergartens, and communes introducing numerous educational innovations, reaching new solutions and responding in more adequate ways to the individual and cultural needs of the child. We should mention here the movement of creative kindergartens. These kindergartens are introducing the elements of whole-language programmes. According to Brian Cutting, they are seeking ways of communicating with parents and using their knowledge and educational experience. Some kindergartens are introducing the ideas of Maria Montessori and Waldorf. However, generally speaking these activities go unnoticed and have no influence on the average kindergarten in Poland.

Research concerning the child during the preschool phase

The following problems will be discussed in this part of the study:

• motives, problems and methodology of the research undertaken

• difficulties with dissemination and impact on practice.

Preparing this study I have undertaken the difficult task of trying to obtain answers to the problems presented above, from the representatives of different academic communities. To my surprise I have noticed a complete lack of publications or other materials popularising the results of research concerning the development and education of the child in the preschool phase. The research to which I will refer could be included in the history of preschool education, in the period before 1987. The failure to place the results of research in the public domain is largely due to changes in the management of the system and the politics of educational research in Poland.

Before I proceed in presenting the results of the survey I need to introduce the institutions which undertake and finance this kind of research in Poland.

There are no institutions in Poland for sponsoring and supervising early childhood education research, although the Ministry of National Education and Science Research Committee (KBN) could be taken into consideration. However, this body does not inspire research questions, as happened in the past. Research concerning the development and education of the small child is only very occasionally financed by the KBN. However, it is not possible to discuss this problem as this institution will not enter into dialogue about the reasons for refusing finance. It could be assumed that the reasons for this situation are the low status of education and especially early childhood education, since there is a general under-investment in this sphere.

However, there have been some favourable changes in relation to the funding of educational research. Sometimes projects are commissioned by publishers or by communes. Research concerning the effectiveness of basic learning conducted earlier at the order of the Institute of Educational Research, by academic teachers of Warsaw University, included projects about the concept of preschool education. This research was carried out in one region of the capital and the project was then repeated on the order of one of the communes (Putkiewicz *et al.*). An ethnographical or ethnomethodological research paradigm was accepted in an attempt to answer the following questions: What experiences is the child having? What is the relation between a child and an adult in this particular socio-cultural context?

One of the significant publishing houses commissioned research concerning the effectiveness of the natural method of learning language. The editor then published manuals for this method and organised training workshops for primary education teachers throughout Poland.

Other examples of projects are those undertaken for Masters theses and PhD degrees in different schools, such as those which train psychologists, pedagogues and teachers in the Vovoidship methodological centres (WOM). Some of these projects seek ways of improving the curriculum, or professionalism in teachers. The results of these research projects are not usually published and remain unknown to a broader community of teachers.

In this field of research, conducted in different academic centres, various paradigms are accepted which to a great extent result from the tradition of the particular community. Often the tradition has been established as the result of research carried out by a well-known researcher. It is said that the Cracow school represented by the Faculty of Psychology of Jagiellonian University, continues a tradition of rigorous research using a clinical model and underpinned by the theories of Piaget. The main research method of the school is fine-grained observation of the phenomena taking place in a given community of children (an example of this school is the work of Szuman *et al.*).

However, a research tradition does not explain the motives for adopting a particular approach, mode of analysis and interpretation of psychological and pedagogical phenomena in other scientific centres. Most centres give priority to research using a positivist approach, starting from theoretical deepening of the problem, hypothesising followed by empirical verification. This approach is typical of the Universities of Warsaw and Poznań.

From the results of the survey, it is difficult to classify according to any particular research paradigm or paradigms. The researchers questioned used different classifications and different criteria from each other. For example, when speaking about research of a positivist type, some mean descriptive research, diagnostic or correlational research which exposes relationships between variables. Others divide the research into the categories 'basic' (pure) and 'applied'. The boundary between them in pedagogical sciences is very fluid and unclear. The ordinary definition of basic research emphasises the lack of direct influence of the results of this research on practice, while in applied research the most important task for the researcher is to effect changes in pedagogical practice.

Such a situation shows on the one hand a varied attitude to research and the variety of paradigms accepted in the research communities. On the other hand the lack of understanding, speaking different languages about the same problems, and the lack of uniform and precise qualification criteria have been highlighted.

In other words, there is no consensus in Polish educational research circles about this question. Until recently there was a conviction that 'pure' research was superior to applied research. Centres carrying out research of this kind were considered 'more scientific' and were granted a higher rank than those engaged in applied research. Consequently they were given higher funds for functioning and for research work. However, 'pure' research does not have a practical application. The differentiation between theoretical and practical research sanctioned the existing differentiation between pedagogical theory and pedagogical practice and what resulted from this divide. Thus such research contributed very little to the improvement of learning, practice and teaching.

The analysis of responses to the survey conducted for this chapter indicates the existence of definite trends in research questions. The respondents mentioned the following problems and issues:

- questions concerning educational activities which create a feeling of personal involvement on the part of adults (parents, teachers) and the child in the process of interaction

- linguistic, ecological, and mathematical education
- transition/the adaptation of the child to the kindergarten
- the maturity of the child in kindergarten and school and the relationship with achievements
- diagnosis of individual needs and the teachers' procedures to meet these
- environmental conditions for optimal development
- the effects on educational progress of different content and structure
- Vygotsky's zone of proximal development
- stimulating cognitive development (J. Piaget, J. Bruner)
- young children's spiritual development
- decision-making processes (preferring, predicting) relating to future events, risk-taking on the part of children
- the structural analysis of the child's behaviour in the peer group and in the family (interaction child–child, child–parent)
- the professional and personal development of teachers.

There is no large-scale research in Poland. It is usually carried out on a representative sample of children of a certain age, on a small scale, due to limited funds and the number of the researchers interested. Their results are known only to their academic colleagues in the research community. It seldom happens that publications appear discussing the results. The only publications released are PhD or other theses.

The prestige of educational research is very low due to a number of reasons:

- lack of funds for financing the research
- under-investment in preschool education
- the low status of early years education in the opinion of both decision-makers and society.

The motives for undertaking research usually result from the researcher's own interests, the sources of which are varied; for instance, the researcher's own theoretical and practical experiences; perceived faults of practice in contrast to their own theoretical knowledge; conflict between the values of the researcher and the values inherent in educational ideology.

Sometimes a project is instigated by the interests of a publisher or occasionally a publication (as with this chapter). Mostly, however, researchers are motivated by personal intellectual needs and these in a way typify their interests and social expectations, as well as their theoretical and methodological training.

The same is true of the researchers' chosen strategies and approaches. Sometimes these will depend on topical research questions. As the age of six to seven years is when children transfer to primary school, it is of concern to parents – six-year-olds are seen as a group at risk and are generally of social interest. However, one researcher respondent stated that 'Children of six to ten years of age are not the object of research and even if they are, the research deals only with the cognitive sphere. Pedagogical research deals with didactic effects.' But younger children (three-year-olds) are not usually the object of research either. If they are, the research is mainly concerned with adaptation to the kindergarten.

In previous years a lot of research was carried out concerning the consequences of growing up in different settings; for example, differences between urban and rural childhoods. This kind of research was demanded by the ruling ideology of social justice. In fact the results had little effect on the standards of living of these children. There were unsuccessful efforts to compensate for environmental deficiencies (additional points granted to children coming from the country during the entrance examination for university places). Such activities freed the government of the time from the need to attend to the reasons for the differences in educational achievements, although they did have a positive social impact (Kwieciński, 1975).

Similarly, there are differences in attainment between rural and urban children at six and seven years old. Attendance at kindergarten has not eradicated the differential level of readiness for school and country children remain disadvantaged (Wilgocka-Okoń, 1972).

The above reflections lead on directly to the role of the value system which underpins research analysis. In Polish research, values have weak scientific status, and research is regarded as mainly concerned with value-free cause and effect relationships between phenomena, open to objective analysis. However, values are certainly the basis for selecting and thinking about a problem, they direct reflections and the interpretation of research results. Often values, as expressed by the education policy of a given government, are covertly accepted by a research community, when in reality there is a need to oppose and problematise them.

The most popular research methods according to respondents are different kinds of observation and interviews, and occasionally standardised tests of development conducted in conjunction with naturalistic observation. There is currently a lack of longitudinal research which would provide data about development processes and the effects of different socio-cultural and environmental conditions.

One of those surveyed suggested there is a need for closer connections between theoretical and research groups dealing with preschool education, through exchange and discussion about basic concepts such as 'childhood', 'development', 'activity' and 'culture', and sharing the results of theoretical and empirical analyses. On the whole researchers are not interested in the dissemination and application of their own research results and practitioners could not afford to buy expensive publications of results. As I have mentioned earlier there is no link between theoreticians and practitioners who would deal with promoting the research results. The people who conduct research have no particular professional competencies in dissemination, nor do they have time to undertake such tasks. However, sometimes research does have an effect on practice, on a small scale. This happened as a result of research carried out several years ago concerning illness in orphans – the findings were later taken into consideration when institutes for the care and education of small children (children's homes, hospitals) were reorganised.

The results of research on a macro-social scale are seldom implemented due to financial reasons. The research community feels generally excluded from macro- or ecosystem-level decisions. But pedagogical innovations on a micro-social scale or in a given region are the consequence of empirical research, more frequently than at macro-level.

Examples of research in child development and early education

The research carried out by Barbara Bokus belongs to the trend of research concerning social interactions of the child with adults and the child with peers in the kindergarten. In her study she dealt with one of the aspects of this process in different configurations: child–child–adult. She answers the question of how children develop interactions, and she tries to create a theoretical model of interaction building between children and adults (Bokus 1984).[5] On the basis of the analysis of many observations conducted with the help of video recordings, the research suggests that a significant role in this process is played by the child's perception of their own activity in initiating interactions and the influence of the partner with whom these interactions are developed. Bokus also explains the phenomenon of diversified usage of language by the child in initiating interactions with peers. The observations covered children from three to five years of age attending kindergarten, in free-play activity (child–child).

The streams of activity of the interaction in the dyad were analysed. The results of the research showed that the establishment of social interactions by a small child cannot be treated as a single act on the child's part which opens a chain of interactions. The process is in fact very complex, consisting of behaviour initiating interactions; for example, the child and partner sharing the same field of attention, or activity in the fun space. Sometimes utterances which opened interaction differed, depending on the distance conceived of as a co-ordination of the two lines of activities in which the child and the partner (whether adult or child) were engaged. The children were found to initiate interactions mostly by drawing their partner into their own activities.

This type of research is of particular importance for those working with disturbed children and those who have difficulties in developing and maintaining interactions in a social environment.

Another research trend concerns problems relating to the diagnosis and analysis of disturbances in children aged between four and seven years old. Barbara Kaja (1987) elaborated the strategy used by therapists and evaluated its effectiveness. The problem of diagnosis of so-called perception disorders and socio-emotional disorders, which interfere with the acquisition of writing and reading abilities in the preschool phase, is noticed very clearly by teachers, psychologists and therapists. All agree that early diagnosis and correction activities can prevent later complex disorders of a different nature.

The author constructed research tools which could be used by workers at a clinic and by teachers in kindergartens, so that the child's behaviour could be observed and analysed in the natural environment. The schedules directed the teacher's observation at the way the child regulates the relations with the surroundings, e.g. do emotional

---

[5] Although the research was carried out much earlier than the given time period for this book it is included here as a model and representative example of psychological basic research.

reactions of the child to the typical kindergarten situation differ in a negative way from the reactions of the remaining peers? On the basis of the teacher's assessments some children were selected for further study. At the next stage of the process 7,867 children aged from four to seven were covered by the diagnostic research. It was found that 16 per cent of children have disorders; 17 per cent of children have difficulties when starting primary school. The author suggested an education-therapeutic method which embraced two areas of influence on the child; one indirect area of influence through advice for parents and one direct area of influence by a personal therapeutic contact with a child.

The author suggests it is unjustified to expect the disorders to disappear spontaneously. Thus there is a need to improve the methods of therapeutic-educational work and introducing this to the kindergarten is a factor in helping the educational process.

Research connected with learning to read and write by children at preschool age is undertaken by many researchers in Poland. Since 1978 reading, writing and maths have been introduced to the preschool programme. Practitioners and theoreticians try to find out more efficient and appropriate methods of working with children in these areas of the curriculum.

The problem of readiness for reading and improving methods of teaching writing with preschool children was discussed by Anna Brzezińska in her research (1987). It is her opinion that motivation and curiosity are the most important ingredients. The development of readiness to read and write is the development of readiness to master a new way of communication with the help of writing – established graphic signs. The child is more and more ready to receive the meaning in such an indirect way, and later to convey meaning and transfer it to others. The author distinguishes five main stages of mastering of this 'new language' – writing:

1. the stage of the development of expression and non-verbal and preverbal communication

2. the stage of the development of expression and verbal communication

3. the stage of discovering signs and their role in the contacts of people among each other

4. the stage of discovering the essence of writing

5. the stage of readiness to control reading and writing.

Brzezińska distinguishes three types of readiness:

1. psychomotoric readiness – 'I know how'

2. vocabulary-notion readiness – 'I have the possibility'

3. emotional-motivational – 'I want'.

In her research she answers questions concerning the level and structure of readiness to read and write of children 4–7 years of age and connections of selected features characterising the child and the family environment with three types of readiness for reading and writing. Finally, the author states that the main factors independent of age, type of social environment and kind of readiness were: the system of communication with the child in the family, the level of manual speed, the short-term memory and verbal productivity.

One of the few large-scale projects conducted by the University of Warsaw concerned differences in school achievement between girls and boys at the age of 9. The researchers analysed data collected in the course of a project on the quality of early education in Poland in 1995 and 1996. They analysed achievement at school in mathematics in four types of social environments: three urban enclaves (740 pupils), distinguished with respect to the parents' SES (parent level of education), and one rural enclave (130 pupils). The test of achievement in mathematics examined basic arithmetic abilities, solving text problems and solving equations. The results obtained point to a clear social involvement of the problem of differences in the achievement of boys and girls. The differences in mathematical achievement of boys and girls vary in the various social enclaves. In the town, the achievement of the girls from the families of low SES are clearly higher than the achievement of boys. In the families of high and middle SES, differences between the achievement of boys and girls are small and equal zero, generally for the benefit of girls. Mathematical achievement of boys is higher in the rural environment (in a traditional rural culture the value of education is higher in relation to the boys). Similarly, though with reversed results in the maths, in the city, some pupils engage in self-fulfilling prophecies relating to 'bad pupils' (usually boys).

Another project asked: in what ways are the features of the child, the kindergarten and the family the instigators of the child's achievements? The research carried out in Poland by Karwowska-Struczyk and others is part of a comparative, longitudinal study being run in 15 countries all over the world under the auspices of IEA and the High/Scope Educational Research Foundation. The PPP (Pre-Primary

Project) is based on the ecological model of development set forth by Bronfenbrenner. This model recognises the complex interplay not only of humans and the environment, but also of various environmental factors. The comparative study as a whole draws on ecological perspectives to explore the interplay of the following groups of variables:

- family characteristics, e.g. parental education – SES; household composition; beliefs about importance of various areas of development for four-year-olds, parental expectations about child's level of education (aspiration and real estimation)

- preschool setting characteristics, e.g. teacher education, experience and age; equipment and materials; group size and adult–child ratio; parental involvement

- elementary school characteristics, e.g. teachers' age, education, experience; group size; parental involvement

- teacher characteristics, e.g. beliefs about importance of various areas of development for four-year-olds; management of children's time; behaviour/interaction with children

- child behaviour, e.g. activities engaged in the setting; involvement with other children; involvement with adults

- child characteristics, e.g. age, gender, SES

- child development status, e.g. cognitive, language, socio-emotional, pre-academic and fine motor development at age 4 and 7.

The Pre-Primary Project consists of three phases at the international level but Poland took part in only two. Phase 1 (1989–1992) could not be carried out in Poland for political reasons. Phase 2 (1992–1993) uses extensive observational and interview data to examine the interactions of child–teacher and to explore the effects of the programme and family factors in children's developmental status at age 4. Phase 3 (1993–1997) completes the project by examining the relationship between early childhood experiences at age 4 and children's development status at age 7.

The accepted research model 'person-process-context' emphasises the meaning of the child's parents, teachers, characteristics, that is, people who are important for the child in determining positive or negative influence of variables of the mezo-, exo- and macrosystem on the character of the processes inside the family and kindergarten affecting the development of the child. Stress is placed on the interplay between characteristic features of the family and the processes within it; characteristic features of kindergarten and school; and the features of the child entangled in the broader systemic variables at the level of exo-, mezo- and macrosystem (Bronfenbrenner, 1992).

Two basic questions were asked:

1. Is the development of the seven-year-old connected with the development features of the four-year-old functioning in two microsystems, i.e. family home and kindergarten?

2. How is the development of the child in the two main microsystems connected with the variables constituting these microsystems and how do they condition these processes?

In the survey we asked about variables influencing the child in two microsystems, remembering that a child is not only their product, but also an actor influencing the systems itself. Attention should be paid to the fact that a number of variables characterising kindergarten and the child's family at four and seven have their roots in meso-, exo- and macrosystems.

The results of the research permit the formulation of several conclusions, one being that a child's development attending kindergarten in the town or in the country has no linear character. We cannot speak about the effects of development as constant variation, nor as changing depending simply on the changes in the child and the environment in which it is developing.

Bronfenbrenner's thesis was confirmed in that statistical treatment of a child's environment, not showing the dynamics of living and growing in a context, is too general and superficial an approach. The analyses of the results of this project are exciting and complex. They provide an attempt to understand whether certain principles and research methods can be applied across national boundaries to help us understand our own and each other's societies, childhoods and education systems better.

References

Bokus, B. (1984) Nawizywanie interakcji spoecznych przez mae dziecko. (*Building up Social Interactions by a Small Child*). Psychological Monographs. T. Tomaszewski (ed.) Vol. XLVII.

Bronfenbrenner, U. (1992) Ecological systems theories, in Ross Vasta, *Six Theories of Child Development: Devised Formulations and Current Issues.* London: Jessica Kingsley.

Bruner, J. (1990) Life as narrative. *Kwartalnik Pedagogiczny,* Vol. 4 no. 138, Warsaw, PWN, p. 5.

Brzeziñska, A. (1987) *Gotowo œ æ dzieci w wieku przedszkolnym do czytania i pisania* (*Readiness of Preschool Children for Reading and Writing*). Poznañ: Adam Mickiewicz University.

Dolata, R., Murawska, B., Putkiewicz, E. and Zytho, M. (1997) *Monitorawanie osiagniçé szkolnych jako metoda doskonalenia edukacji* (*Monitoring of School Achievements as the Method of Achieving of Education*). Warszawa: Zak.

Dolata, R., Murawska, B., Putkiewicz, E. and Zytho, M. (1997) Mathematical achievements of children: where should we look for differences in achievements of girls and boys, paper prepared for the 7th European Conference on the Quality of Early Childhood Education, Munich, 1997.

Janion, M. (1996) *Czy bêdziesz wiedziad co prze¿yeœ?* (*Would you know what you had felt?*). Warsaw: ed. Sic.

Kaja, B. (1987) *The Problems of the Diagnosis in and Therapy for Disturbances in Children at Preschool Age*. Bydgoszcz: WSP.

Karwowska-Struczyk, M., Bielen, B. and Malkowska-Zegadlo, H. (1997), Zwiaski miedsy doswiadczeniami i kompetencjami nabywanymi w zrózni-cowanych srodowiskack wychowawczych przez dzieci w wieku 4 lat a poziomem rozwoju wybranych kompetencji tych w wieku 7 lat, (Relations between experience and competencies acquired by 4-year-olds in different socialising microsystems and developmental status of those children at age 7), Warszawa, IBE (unpublished).

Kwieciñski, Z. (1975) Erodowisko a wyniki pracy szkoy (Environment and School Results), Warsaw, APN, IRWiR.

Miller, R. *Dostêp do oœwiaty i wyrównywanie startu szkolnego. Problem wêz³owy* (*Access to the Education and Levelling of the School Start. Key Problems*).

Szuman, S. (1985), Dziela wybrane; Studia nad rozwojem psychicznym dziecka, Vol. 1; Podstawy rozwoju I wychowanie w ontogenezie, Vol. 2. Warszawa: WSiP.

Wilgocka-Okoñ, B. (1972) *Dojrzaoœæ szkolna dzieci a œrodowisko* (*Children's School Maturity and the Environment*). Warsaw.

Wilgocka-Okoñ, B. (1989) *Stan wychowania przedszkolnego w Polsce* (*The State of Preschool Education in Poland*). Topics Report, 16. Warsaw-Cracow: PWN.

Wood, A. (1990) The need for community mobilisation: past experience and future needs, in Betty Po-King Chan (ed.) *Early Childhood Education Toward the Twenty-First Century. a worldwide perspective.* Hong Kong and Gaithersburg, MD: Yew Chung Education Publishing Company.

8

Early Childhood Education: Research in Spain

Teresa Aguado and Rosario Jimenez Frias

Introduction

Pedagogical research focusing on the non-compulsory stage of education (0–6 years) has been an almost non-existent concern in our country until very recently, mainly due to the fact that this period of education was not the subject of pedagogical reflection in the strict sense. The main purpose of educational institutions for children of this age was to provide assistance, and act as a continuation of the home and the family, the object being to care for and rear children. One of the consequences of this state of affairs was a lack of thorough research into the educational process at this stage, providing analysis and data beyond that of the merely descriptive type.

The political transition and the democratisation of teaching that began in the 1970s was a decisive inflexion point in education policy. One of the targets to be achieved is to extend the scope of preschool education (how it should be carried out, with what age groups, what professional staff), and the most suitable educational practice at this level is beginning to be questioned. Some studies have been produced based on theoretical premises derived from theories on development processes; teaching layouts were designed; new interests and formulas were proposed for training teachers; the relationship between school and the community was strengthened; and preparing for the transition from preschool to compulsory schooling was attended to (Martin Moreno and Frontera Sancho, 1977).

The curriculum policy that arose out of the Education Reform (Ministry of Education and Science, 1988/1996) vindicated that the specific nature of the 0–6-year-old period was as an educational and contextualisation stage, which was not subordinate to compulsory schooling. The educational innovation model used by the Ministry of

111

Education and Science for implementing the Reform of the Educational System, and, thus, the infant education level, is known in general terms as research/experiment/dissemination, in which basic theories and data are used to generate ideas which are then turned into prototypes that have to be put to the test, redesigned and retested. It states as one of its guidelines the examination of the various elements that comprise the system, preparing the right criteria and tools, and comparing results in accordance with the principles and functions that have been developed (Aguado, 1993). As a result of this change in educational policy, there has been an increase of official funding for research projects focusing on infant education. Funds for carrying out research into this level of education come mainly from two financial sources connected to the Ministry of Education and Science. The INCIE network, during the 1970s, and the Centre for Educational Research and Documentation (CIDE), from the 1980s onwards. The latter regularly offers both grants for educational research and research project contests. The Centre for Childhood and Family Studies, which depends on the Ministry of Social Affairs, backs work dealing with the problems involved in family education (La educación familiar en los primeros años, Madrid: CEMF, 1995).

The university departments of faculties of education and psychology, using their own resources, stimulate and finance research carried out by teams of teachers and scholarship students. Private funding is scarce. For the work carried out for this paper, we were only able to find funds from the Fundación Santa Maria and the Spanish delegation of OMEP (World Organisation for Preschool Education).

Researchers: training and status

Any research that has been acknowledged as such, and which has any likelihood of being published, has lain almost exclusively in the hands of those professionals who are considered to be suitably qualified, i.e. university teachers and staff connected to various official organisations. Investigation and thought from preschool teachers themselves has rarely been officially accepted and disseminated as research. There are several reasons for this, including the fact that there is the usual division between practice, on the one hand, and theory and researchers, on the other, at a level that had so far never been granted its own educational status. Teacher training was mostly aimed at childcare, as an extension of the parental and family role, instead of providing intellectual resources and customs that would encourage thought and investigation into actual practice. The layering of the educational system, its selective and hierarchic nature, is once again seen in the status given to the pre-compulsory stage of education.

The division between researchers into education and its practitioners is one of the symptoms that define the Spanish educational panorama. This state of affairs cultivates the obvious reticence they feel towards one another. It is due to the lack of research training for practitioners, and the encouragement of research elitism in those considered as experts. The plans for research and action that are a feature of other contexts similar to our own, are a long way off from becoming part of the professional culture of Spanish educational research. The approximation of theory and practice has come about – as in the author's own case – thanks to professionals involved in the 0–6-year-old level (teachers, educators, teacher trainers) who have acquired the status of researchers through professional promotion, obtaining doctorates and occupying university chairs, whence they promote lines of research dealing with this level of education, and which encourage the participation of the professionals working directly at this level. Exceptions to this rule usually involve university professors with previous experience at different levels of education who transmit in their research papers their concern for overcoming the false and futile division between theory and practice. These are the people who are trying to illustrate inter-disciplinary and inter-level research projects.

Some issues still pending include the modification of the actual professional background of infant educators by appropriate theoretical and methodological training that will provide them with the right tools for entering into a fluent and rewarding dialogue with university experts. The latter, officially recognised, researchers, should have a better response to the concerns and questions that arise in practice. A common code must be created, a language not only of concepts and meanings but also questions to be resolved in co-operation.

Theoretical models

The theoretical models that comprise the framework for research correspond to development models upon which the projects and plans of action for this level of education have been based: the maturationist model, the cultural transmission model, and the cognitive-constructivist model. The underlying values of the maturationist model are centred on the defence of individual freedom and stress humanist ethics that place the emphasis on children's rights and happiness. In the cultural transmission model, the priority is the acquisition of power and social status through success in school. School is selective and forms the intellectual 'elite'. The cognitive development model is centred around universal ethical and cognitive elements. Genetic epistemology provides descriptions of psychological states in terms of progress towards better moral and cognitive reasoning (Piaget, 1932/1965; Kohlberg, 1982).

Two very different points are to be seen if we analyse the theoretical basis from which research and action at this level have been approached. Until experimentation and introduction of the Education Reform, the 0–6-year-old level was explained using models that were almost exclusively maturationist, particularly for 0–3 years of age. This was in response to a development theory based on maturity, and meant accepting that the most important part of a child's development comes from inside that person. Hence, given the right psychological, physical and nutritional environment, a child reaches each stage of his or her growth according to a predetermined scheme.

The second level of infant education (3–6 years old), particularly the last year, is regarded as preparation for school, and obvious priority is given to the approach based on cultural transmission, which uses mechanistic explanations for development. This connects with the mechanistic and programmed learning theories (Mayer, 1971; Decker and Decker, 1984; Aguado, 1993). Their epistemological position reflects the empiricist tradition that assumes knowledge to be a result of information from outside the individual reaching his or her inside via the senses.

Two strategies are used to define educational objectives (Aguado, 1993):

1. accepting school knowledge and behaviour patterns along with those which predict 'success', power and social status

2. using the academic contents of psychometric and other tests.

In this context, learning implies a visible change in behaviour, something that can be gauged. Teachers define the type of behaviour to be achieved and they direct, increase or modify the response. A series of abilities is designed by analysing the kinds of initial skills and conditions required to perform a task (Allen, 1972). Learning to read and write, do maths, or be able to understand scientific concepts, are all basic skills according to this approach, because success at school is believed to help ensure success in professional life.

The learning process is conceived as a visible and directly measurable change in behaviour that leads the pupil from the simple to the complex and from the specific to the abstract, by analysing tasks in a logical manner (Stevens and King, 1987). The stages or phases of the learning process (Gagné, 1974; Peters, Neisworth and Yawkey, 1985) are:

1. motivating the pupil to become actively involved in the task

2. focusing the pupil's attention on relevant aspects of the material and the activity

3. helping pupils to learn the material they are taught

4. ensuring that what is learnt is remembered

5. generalisation, or transferring what is learnt to fresh situations

6. stimulating pupils to try to obtain the best results in learning.

The Education Reform and the official documents that describe and illustrate it proposed a new theoretical orientation which explains and justifies practice and thought in the 0–6 age group. This is known as the cognitive orientation model and explains infant development as a dialectic process shared among genes and environment, nature and upbringing. The five major influences in development are maturation, or main genetic factors; experience or environmental inputs; tasks by which the individual interacts with his or her environment; consultation with others; and the interaction of all the above (Decker and Decker, 1980). This complies with the semantic model of dialectic process. Children are scientists or philosophers who gradually reorganise their knowledge on the basis of a personal 'reading' of their experience. This metaphor, which Plato examined, was reinterpreted by Hegel and adopted by the educational philosophy of Dewey, Baldwin, Claparede and Piaget. Their strategy for defining goals is based on an internal and formal pattern of adaptation which is not confined to the order of events in time, and which has to be construed as a group of ethical and epistemological principles and justified in ethical and philosophical terms.

It is not so much a question of creating individual teaching designs, as of providing the classroom with enough material so that moments of cognitive restructuration will occur. An open curriculum is used in which the teacher initiates ideas and responses to the children's activities (Weikart, 1972). The essential goal is to improve the scope and depth of development by structuring experience and with confident exploration activity. Contents – cognitive structures, internal schemes, physical, logical-mathematical and social knowledge – are presented in a global manner by setting up learning centres that arouse children's interest and curiosity, along with the desire to learn. The teacher's role is to observe, assess, structure the environment, ask questions and redirect learning. The teacher acts as a companion who minimises the use of authority and control over the children. The teacher guides them, stimulates their enterprise, games, experiments, reasoning and social co-operation (Aguado, 1993).

Research is currently carried out on the basis of eclectic models in which components from the latter two models are taken into account, i.e. the pre-academic and the cognitive-constructivist models.

Current focuses of attention: subjects and methods

Research carried out in the 1970s and 1980s was, typically, of a predominantly descriptive nature, with little methodological thoroughness, large material limitations and a lack of research method training on the behalf of both those responsible and those taking part (Escudero Escorza and Fernandez Uria, 1976). The situation changed over the 1980s and 1990s, and became focused on issues arising from the theoretical models described above – pre-academic and constructivist – and in response to proposals made by the authorities – the integration of pupils with special needs, and the Education Reform (Ministry of Education and Science, 1988/1996). Within this framework of reference there are five areas in which research into the infant education level has been approached.

1. Special education and school integration

Specific alterations have been examined using case studies. Here are some examples:

- Infant cerebral dysfunction (Lafarga and Julian, 1995). A theory is used that involves emotional and educational variable factors, including cognitive flexibility, analysed on the basis of Feuerstein's cognitive model.

- Cerebral palsy (Garcia-Sanchez, Caballero and Castellanos, 1995). The behaviour of various different syndromes of cerebral palsy are assessed using the various sub-scales of the Brunet-Lezine psychomotor development scale at the age of two.

- The hypermedial method of teaching for those with defective hearing (Sierrea Rubio, 1995), the object of which is to use computer technology in teaching children with hearing difficulties to read and write.

- Certain relationship and motor disturbances associated with various deficiencies have been dealt with using early stimulation programmes (0–3-year-olds) as both remedies and care. This was the case of the experience analysed by Taberner, Agote and Aliaga (1995), and which was based on a model of integration that encompassed physical, psychological and social aspects applied by a multi-disciplinary team.

Various areas are involved in the treatment, such as language/communication, motor stimulation and rehabilitation, general stimulation and psychotherapy. The conclusions of the study called attention to the need for action at an early age in risk situations, to prevent altered development and to make it unnecessary for any subsequent and less efficacious remedial action to be taken. One of the obstacles to applying this kind of scheme is the lack of co-ordination between the health/care system and the education/schooling system.

2. *Socio-cultural differences*

The socio-cultural differences that have been analysed in research at this level of infant education mainly concern family education and cultural differences and are illustrated by the following studies:

- The educational strategies used within the family medium are considered a means to achieve the purposes of the preschool level. The methodology used is descriptive and is focused on case studies (Garrido Medina and Gil Calve, 1995).

- The bilingual nature of some Spanish regions has been the subject of attention in terms of its effect on school performance and adaptation. Evidence so far would suggest that preschool education should be given in the mother tongue, as it is important for children to experience the compatibility of the languages coexisting in their environment. The new code is introduced gradually by 'immersion' in the school language (Aguado, 1989; Huguet, 1995).

- From the culturalist point of view, projects are developed on the basis of the idea that school should cater for pupils' cultural differences, not only for axiological or social reasons, but because otherwise the essential purposes will not be achieved, such as building up the child's own personal cultural identity, and equal opportunities for access to the available socio-educational goods and resources, regardless of cultural background.

One example of this last line of investigation is currently under way with the title 'Cultural diversity and school equality: formulation and assessment of a model for action in multicultural educational contexts'. The research is both theoretical and practical. The theoretical side will analyse the educational treatment of cultural diversity from different angles, the concepts of the proposed intercultural education model will be defined, and the evidence collected by research in this field of study will be revised. The practical side of the project aims to provide information on real practice in schools (infant, and compulsory primary and secondary), in order to identify and regulate action that will benefit equal opportunities and educational results, putting the proposed intercultural model to the test.

3. *Diagnosis*

The analysis and preparation of tools for individual diagnosis, mainly related to reading and writing skills, has attracted the attention of a considerable number of researchers, mainly from the field of educational counselling and on the basis of psychometric assumptions. Here are a few:

- The adaptation in Spain of the Martineck and Zaichkowsky (MZSCS, 1977) scale of self-concept scale for girls and boys between 4 and 5 years of age, the purpose being to study the effect of pupils' self-concept in relation to the development of the graphic act of writing (Buisan, 1995).

- Preparing a graphic ability test to establish the levels of learning joined writing, and enabling the child's written work to be situated in each of the copies (Alfaro and Martin, 1995).

- Early identification (4–5 years of age) of potentially gifted pupils in order to plan educational counselling in line with the needs of such pupils (Lopez Andrada, 1991) and to provide teachers with information to help them modify their working habits with such pupils and enable them to improve their ability to identify them (Alvarez, 1996).

4. *Cognitive and learning processes*

The cognitive processes involved in learning have been analysed because of their value as a factor of school success. The attention of researchers, mainly from the field of educational psychology, has been focused on the acquisition of concepts and meta-cognitive aspects, such as the following:

- The formation of concepts has been approached from Piaget's genetic viewpoint, in order to define the models that 4–6-year-olds use to conceptualise (Bernad Mainar, 1983). In a more clinical than psychometrical way, fairly unstructured techniques are used to collect data that can be manipulated with unsophisticated statistical techniques. The conclusions arrived at reveal that the level attained with the conceptualisation process depends on the degree to which the lower level has been carried out: a functional level is attained depending on the extent of figural assimilation that is acquired.

- The oral expression of scientific concepts during the second cycle of infant education (3–6 years old) is dealt with in an ethnographic study that has been developed over six academic years (Pla Molins, 1996). It consists of observing and analysing communicative interaction between schoolchildren and teachers when teaching and learning topics in class, or during workshops that are described as scientific and thematic and which include devising programme units from the physics angle.

- Learning elementary logical structures has been analysed from the constructivist approach (Jimenez Frias, 1987), using work derived from this approach combined with theories on information processing (Vecino, 1996). As a result of this work, didactic models of action have been proposed for the 3–6-year-old age group.

- The causal relationship between developing metaphonological segmentation skills and learning to read has been approached with a training study which defines the relationships between phonological awareness and reading ability (Carillo, 1996).

5. *Programme assessment*

The teaching reform has promoted the devising and assessment of systematic plans of action developed in response to the demands and requirements of fresh educational approaches:

- Educational innovation introduced in the experimental infant education programme (Ministry of Education and Science, 1988/1996) is analysed on the basis of the observations of the teacher involved (Quintero, 1988). The point of this is to discover the extent of knowledge and understanding of the innovations, the degree of internalisation of the proposed changes, and any contextual problems and conditioning factors. The results are alarming, as teaching staff do not consider the changes to be significant and, in most cases, they have been confined to superficially modifying the physical structure of classes, introducing activity 'workshops' or 'corners'. There is a lack of suitable permanent teacher training, support and trouble-shooting systems, and of adequate stuctural adaptation.

- The analysis and assessment of programmes within the experimental scheme for the reform of infant education (3–6-year-olds) are the subject of a longitudinal survey to be carried out over two school years. The aim of this is to identify factors that spell the difference between experimental and non-experimental programmes and which are related to pupils' results in terms of the intended purposes of the reform project (Aguado, 1993). A transversal, longitudinal design is used, applying ad hoc tools suited to the targets of the survey and applying temporal series analysis to assess the changes that occur over time. The results enable us to see significant differences between experimental and non-experimental programmes in the majority of the context and process factors considered. However, there are differences in pupils' results when programmes are compared by groups according to the degree of adaptation to the organizational and educational criteria set out in official documents (Ministry of Education and Science, 1988/1996).

- Applying the added value analysis technique to assess infant education programmes (Castro and Garcia, 1995) enables us to compare the results obtained after the programme had been used, analysing whether or not they are greater than those which may be attributed to maturation. This study confirms the positive effect of action involving cognitive style development, both in groups and individually. There is clearly a need to develop more complex models, better suited to real school life, and some practical ways to define the parameters of this model.

- Multisensorial globalised methodology is proposed as a formula for the 3–6-year-old age group. The purposes as regards pupils are: to contribute to pupils' development as a whole, provide multisensorial stimulation and serve to prevent possible deficiencies. The method aims to provoke and accelerate multiple sensorial development – of both external and internal senses – in order to provide access to thought and mental functions and to facilitate learning skills and abilities. The results of the assessment of this method confirm its positive effects on the sensorial factors analysed (Lebrero, 1995).

Equal opportunities in early childhood education

Equal opportunities at the infant education level are the object of special attention in order to avoid discrimination on the basis of socio-cultural factors, a complex group of factors that influence and modulate all educational activity. These differences arise from the various socio-cultural media that converge in any educational process: the official one, which reflects society as a whole; that of those involved; that of reference communities; that which is actually transmitted in educational interaction. Both the individual and group differences above should be interpreted and assessed according to socio-cultural factors such as socio-economic and professional status, access to social resources, the family and reference community cultural context. There are two approaches upon which specific educational action has been based, adapted according to so-called socio-cultural differences: compensation and culture. The former accepts that socially acquired shortcomings do exist, while the latter deals with culturally formed differences.

Compensation proposals

These proposals are aimed at achieving equal opportunities using differential treatment based on models that explain school failure in terms of environmental shortcomings. Educational compensation developed over the last thirty years in the USA and Spain is aimed at raising the level of academic performance in underprivileged groups, in accordance with the renewed concept of equal opportunities in education. Coherent with the deficit models upon which they are based, additional educational programmes and services have been devised which are aimed at educational rehabilitation and at widening educational opportunities for disadvantaged groups and/or those running a risk of school failure – groups which are, for financial, cultural, physical or psychological reasons, in unequal conditions for coping with schooling (European Council, 1977) and which do not therefore benefit from ordinary education (Flaxman, 1985). The programmes include environmental enhancement, early stimulation, continued and consistent educational stimulation, dealing with specific learning difficulties, connecting with the school curriculum, organising media and resources, and family support (Lazaro, Swan and Rosemnige, 1983). It is a form of positive discrimination that favours pupils with restricted educational opportunities due to their social and family experience (Espin, 1991).

It is hoped that the school environment will be able to mitigate the negative influence of the socio-cultural environment with pro-grammes and services specifically aimed at raising school results (Ministry of Education and Science, 1988/1996). In spite of the enthu-siasm and expectations of those in charge of some of the projects intro-duced, the assessment of the first compensation strategies, in terms of the efficiency of compensation programmes, show we should lower our initial optimism as, in general, the positive effects were not sus-tained in the long term. There was also a lack of definition of pur-poses and general theories within which to encompass and define the various programmes (Little and Smith, 1971; Espin, 1991; Jimenez 1990). The concept of socio-cultural disadvantage, along with com-pensatory education, was later developed more thoroughly, due to their significance in developing differential educational adaptation in terms of socio-cultural factors.

The term 'socio-cultural disadvantage' – or socio-cultural deficiency or handicap – is used to explain the failure in school of particular groups with specific cultural or social traits (suburban areas, cultural groups, ethnic groups, immigrants, marginal groups). In theory, the term refers to inequalities in the type of educational stimulation provided for some pupils due to their socio-cultural background. It is a static term used to classify groups and individuals who, to one extent or another, deviate from what is considered to be the average model or pattern, when no physical or mental characteristics can be found to justify this distinction. Several criteria have been used to operatively define the term 'socio-cultural disadvantage' (De Miguel, 1984):

- Social class, using parents' social and professional status and level of schooling as a gauge.

- Cultural environment, usually meaning being deprived to some extent of stimulation and experience (Wiseman, 1964; Bloom, 1964; Bereiter and Engelman, 1977).

- Language. This is an underlying factor of the cultural background and is associated with cognitive development. Language and cog-nitive inadequacy should not be associated, as no causal relation-ship has been proven (Stubbs, 1982), although there is some correlation with socialization.

- Intelligence. Sometimes the hereditary nature of this is emphasised, and sometimes the socio-cultural environment. Criteria used to define the term include social class, cultural background, language and intellectual capacity (De Miguel, 1984).

The most recent work on compensatory education emphasises the concern for and thoroughness of the design, application and assessment of long-term programmes. They are less mechanistic and more interested in the pupil's interaction with his or her family, school and community environment. They are aimed at detecting and perfecting cognitive, affective and social strategies, and they value pupils' experiences and culture of origin, strengthening their concept of self. The intended project should be negotiated and accepted by teachers and suited to the specific needs of the community at which it is aimed. Discontinuity between the various different contexts in which pupils are involved should be reduced from an ecological point of view; it should support the right to cultural diversity; prepare the contents of compensatory programmes on the basis of learning skills and prerequisites; provide assessment in terms of both training and criteria; encourage the training of teachers in the design, use and assessment of programmes, developing positive attitudes towards the pupils and targets involved (Espin, 1991).

It has to be stressed that the object pursued should not be compensatory education in itself, but rather an improvement in the standard of the general education of all individuals and groups. A differential integration model (Lopez Lopez, 1990; Stallings and Stipck, 1986) should be used that sees differences as a dynamic relationship between individuals and groups and differential educational intervention as a continued process of adaptation according to the ever-changing conditions that arise due to the interaction of pupils' own characteristics and educational situations. The evidence would appear to indicate the following (Jimenez Fernandez, 1987):

(a) There is no proof of the alleged linguistic, intellectual or cultural inferiority of subjects from underprivileged classes.

(b) It is wrong to set up comparisons on the basis of discriminatory procedures and tools based on cultural/linguistic variations, emphasis on cognitive and academic ones, and on performance rather than process.

(c) The social class factor must be redefined, using indicators better suited to social reality.

(d) A differential analysis should be made, avoiding any preliminary assessment on the basis of allegedly ideal norms or patterns.

(e) There is a lack of co-ordination between the family and the school cultural medium, and this is made clear by the differences in expectations, beliefs, practices, meaning and values conveyed to the pupil by both.

(f) It is considered necessary to analyse the degree of intercultural continuity/discontinuity, cultural separation, and their relationship to school failure.

A multidimensional and systematic approach should be adopted by using a behavioural, cognitive and ecological paradigm: analysing the precise nature of the relationship between behaviour and environment and identifying potential mediators between the two; reconstruing and analysing the cultural factors that modulate the educational process.

Along these lines, the recent Royal Decree on action to be taken in compensation for inequality (1996) in compliance with Chapter V of Law 1/1990 on the Organisation of the General Education System, aims to regulate the measures which enable us to forecast and compensate for inequality in education derived from social, economic, cultural, geographic, ethnic or any other factor. It is also aimed at strengthening the ordinary measures that exist within the education system and promoting other, extraordinary, ones. In order to fulfil these intended purposes, the Spanish Ministry of Education and Science proposes, amongst other measures, the following:

> Increasing the supply of school places in the second cycle of infant education (3–6 years old), guaranteeing access to pupils from rural areas and disadvantaged pupils to educational services and resources. Encouraging early school attendance, with the co-operation of other administrative bodies and institutions. (Ministry of Education and Science, 1988/96, Art. 6)

> At the infant education level (0–6 years), action aimed at educational compensation will be of a preventive nature and will be governed by the principle of standardisation, avoiding the use of any organisational formulae in the teaching/learning process that involve segregation. (ibid., Art. 12)

Among the official measures for promoting educational research, the offers of research grants organised by the Ministry of Education and Science are of particular importance. The last offer (at the time of writing this had been in March 1996) gave priority to three issues, including those referring to compensation for educational inequalities.

The culturalist approach

Adopting this approach means overcoming a restrictive and marginalising approach by defining the various social groups – women, children, the young, the elderly, immigrants, linguistic or religious minorities, rural or suburban populations, etc. – by using a differential approach to identify and deal with the specific cultural nature that they each represent. A line of thought and action has therefore been devised known as multicultural and/or intercultural education, based on philosophical, sociological, anthropological, psychological and pedagogical assumptions, amongst others. On the basis of these approaches, a multicultural educational proposal has been designed which is interwoven with all the above, and may be defined as follows:

> An educational approach based on the respect and value of cultural diversity, aimed at all members of society as a whole, that proposes a model of action that is both formal and informal, holistic and integrated, and which shapes all the aspects of the educational process in order to achieve equal opportunities and results, overcome racism in its various shapes and forms, and obtains intercultural communication and skill. (Aguado, 1996)

It is an angle from which to confront issues involving how to deal with cultural diversity in education. It is understood that this diversity can be seen beyond the limits of race, or ethnic and national groups, and that it interacts with other significant factors both in terms of educational action in formal education contexts and in other, less structured, informal ones. Equal opportunities and resources mean that skills, talents and experiences are considered as a suitable starting point for subsequent schooling and require justice and a real chance to obtain equal results for a greater number of pupils. It implies a balance between the formal and informal, individuals and groups, process and product, diversity and unity. It requires co-ordination between processes of change, a positive self-image, self-confidence and self-affirmation. It requires clarity to confront dilemmas and paradoxes. By adopting measures that benefit equal opportunities we put to the test our capacity for tolerance, along with our appreciation of diversity as a valuable strength and not a weakness to be overcome. It is important that schools adopt measures that benefit these equal opportunities, but it is just as important that equality be defended in all steps that are taken in the realm of work, family and society.

The Multicultural Education proposal is ambitious in its targets insofar as it involves adopting an approach that modulates all educational decisions while promoting differentiated action according to the interaction of cultural variables and other significant factors in education. Its efficacy will depend to a great extent on this action being coherent with individual and community needs analysis within the specific context into which it is introduced: but it will also depend upon being combined with other structural measures outside the realm of school. If these conditions are not fulfilled, so-called multicultural initiatives may be used to camouflage inequality, or as an alibi to avoid adopting ideas that truly respect cultural diversity, or even as a showcase for the more 'touristic' and superficial view of cultural manifestations.

Outlooks and proposals

Studies should be promoted aimed at overcoming the conceptual, personal and methodological limitations that have been noted throughout this review including the following:

1. Infant education issues still occupy an outside place as far as basic and fundamental scientific lines of thought are concerned, and which standardise and monopolise the building up and legitimisation of knowledge, both in content and method.

2. The demographic features of university teachers and researchers, most of whom are male, along with their professional culture, do not make it easy to introduce preschool issues as legitimate ones.

3. Formal and informal investigation into research methods benefit and give priority to studying certain issues and using certain methods as opposed to others. Academic expectations, even today, rarely include the preschool level.

4. Funds for studies in this area are, as a general rule, still very limited. The current situation in this area in Spain will be shown below. Amongst other ideas, there are several projects that are being developed thanks to research grants from the Educational Research and Documentation Centre.

Some suggestions for designing and developing coherent studies would be:

1. Using *multicultural approaches* in research design and methodology; preparing combined and complex designs which use, at all levels of the research process, diverse methods which, even at risk of par-

tial overlapping, would complement and strengthen each other and provide quantitative and qualitative data, appropriate information on the context, and the experience of those involved. It would be necessary to use both quasi-experimental and experimental designs, ethnographic research, ex-post-facto, case studies and non-reactive research.

2. Using strategies based on a *multimethodological* approach, acknowledging the fact that different research methods provide potential solutions for different problems. Solutions and answers to problems and questions that arise during research should be sought, using a variety of methods which, even if they partially overlap, complement each other and ensure greater thoroughness and reliability in results.

3. Compiling more and more refined *research models* to cater mainly for studying educational factors that describe and modulate the teaching/learning process (pupils' mental processes, teacher/pupil interaction), indicated by social groups theory and expectation theory (Rosenthal and Jackobson, 1968), and affective variables such as concept of self, school/home relationship, adaptation to the community, the family, school, community attitudes.

4. Monitoring the *results of programmes* and action in infant education in a systematic and consistent way; consulting parents and teachers, allowing them to participate in the educational decision-making process; overcoming deficit models and supporting teacher training; identifying differences between various educational models and programmes using relevant criteria.

5. Overcoming the dichotomy between educational theory and practice, and asking relevant questions for improving action during the preschool level, refining the media and methods used and facilitating the application of research results.

6. Designing, applying and *assessing initial and permanent training programmes* for teachers and other professionals. Preparing and providing materials and resources among teachers, schools, programmes, support teams and social services.

An example would be to put together a multidisciplinary team – university teachers from various fields, professionals from formal and informal education, local and community institutions – in a quest for adequate solutions to the pupils' own needs and those of their families, based on diverse outlooks, approaches and methodology.

References

Aguado, T. (1989): Influencia del bilingüismo en el rendimiento escolar. Estudio de un caso. *Actas de Y Jornadas de Pedagogia Diferencial.* UNED, Madrid, pp. 65–80.

Aguado, T. (1993) *Análisis y evaluación de modelos y programas de educación infantil en el marco de la Reforma de la Enseñanza.* Madrid: Cuadernos de la UNED, no. 124, UNED.

Aguado, T. (1996) *Educación Multicultural: su teoría y su práctica.* Madrid: Cuadernos de la UNED, UNED.

Alfaro, I. and Martin, B. (1995) Escalas gráficas por edad del test de aptitud grafica L/S cursiva. *Estudios de investigación educativa en intervención psicopedagógica.* VII Seminario Nacional de Modelos de Investigación Educativa. Valencia: AIDIPE, pp. 333–6.

Allen, D. (1972) Health Education: Utilization of infant auto restraints. *Pediatrics*, Vol. 58, pp. 323–8.

Alvarez, A. (1990): Diseño cultural: Una aproximación ecológica a la educación desde el paradigma histórico-cultural. In *Infancia y Aprendizaje*, 51–2, 41–77.

Alvarez, B. (1996) *Programas de enriquecimiento para alumnos biendotados de cinco a siete años.* Proyecto de Tesis Doctoral, Madrid, UNED.

Banks, J. A. (1991) Multicultural education: its effects on students' racial and gender role attitudes, in J. P. Shaver (ed.) *Handbook of Research on Social Studies Teaching and Learning.* New York: Macmillan.

Bereiter, C. and Engleman, S. (1977) *Enseñanza especial preescolar.* Fontanella, Barcelona. Bernad Mainar, J. A. (1983) Formación de conceptor en niñer de 4 a 6 años. ICE, Universidad de Zaragoza.

Bloom, B. S. (1964) *Stability and Change in Human Characteristics.* Wiley, New York.

Buisan, C. (1995) La escala de autoconcepto para niños y niñas de 4 y 5 años: un estudio en una muestra catalana. *Estudios de investigación educativa en intervención psicopedagógica.* VII Seminario Nacional de Modelos de Investigación Educativa. Valencia: AIDIPE, pp. 200–2.

Carillo, S. (1996) *La relación causal entre el desarrollo de las habilidades metafonológicas de segmentación y la adquisicin de la lectura.* Research project Madrid: CYGT.

Castro, M. and Garcia, M. (1995) Análisis del valor añadido como técnica alternativa en la evaluación de programas de educación infantil. *Estudios de investigación educativa en intervención psicopedagógica.* VII Seminario Nacional de Modelos de Investigación Educativa. Valencia: AIDIPE, pp. 218–23.

CEMF (1995): La educación familiar en los primeros años. Madrid.

Decker, C. A. and Decker, J. R. (1984) *Planning and Administering Early Childhood Education.* Columbus: Merril.

De Miguel, A. (1984): Investigación en torno a la educación compensatoria. *Revista de Investigación Educativa*, Vol. 2, No. 3, pp. 41–58.

Escudero Escorza, T. and Fernández Uria, C. (1976): Investigación educativa. Informe INCIE/MEC.

Espín, J. (1991): Los programas de educación compensatoria. ¿Una respuesta a las diferencias socioculturales desde la educación? C. Jiménez Fernández, *Lectures de Pedagogía Diferencial*. Dykinson: Madrid, pp. 105–34.

Flaxman, E. (1985): *Comprehensive Education*. Husen y T. N. Postlethwait (eds): *The International Encyclopedia of Education*. Pergamon, Oxford, pp. 507–30.

Gagné, R. M. (1974) *The Conditions of Learning*, Holt-Rinehart and Wilson: New York.

García Sánchez, J. L., Gaballero, P. and Castellanos, T. (1995) Sindromes cerebrales y conducta adaptativa. *Estudios de investigción educativa en intervención psicopedagógica*. VII Seminario Nacional de Modelos de Investigación Educativa. Valencia. AIDIPE, pp. 105–10.

Garrido Medina, S. and Gil Calvo, A. (1995): *Educación familiar y escolar*. Estudios de investigación educativa en intervención psicopedagógica. VII Seminario Nacional de Modelos de Investigación Educativa. Valencia, AIDIPE, pp. 136–47.

Gimeno Sacristan, J. (1991) Curriculum y diversidad cultural. *11°Jornadas de Enseñantes de Gitanos*. Valencia, 4 September.

Huguet, A. (1995): Conocimiento lingüístico de los escolares de la Franja Oriental de Aragón e implicaciones curriculares del tratamiento de las lenguas. Doctoral thesis. Universidad de Lleida.

Jimenez Fernandez, C. (1987) *Cuestiones sobre bases diferanciales de la educación*. Unidades Didacticas. Madrid: UNED.

Jimenez Frias, R. A. (1987) *La adquisición de las estructuras logicas elementales*. Doctoral thesis. Madrid: Universidad Complutense.

Jiménez Frías, R. A. (1990) Pedagogía Diferencial. Educación preescolar. UNED, Madrid.

Kohlberg, L. (1982) Estadios morales y moralización. El enfoque cognitivo-evolutivo. *Infancia y Aprendizaje*, Vol. 18, pp. 33–51.

Lafarga, M. and Julian, J. J. (1995) Análisis de un caso de disfunción cerebral infantil. *Estudio de investigación educativa en intervención psicopedagógica*. VII Seminario Nacional de Modelos de Investigación Educativa. Valencia: AIDIPE, pp. 97–101.

Lázaro, B; Swan, T. and Rosemnige, A. (1985): Compensatory Education. En T. Husen y T. N. Postlethwait (eds.) *The International Encyclopedia of Education*. Pergamon: Oxford, pp. 607–32.

Lebrero, M. P. (1995) *Educación Infantil (2° ciclo)*. Madrid: Fundación Santa Maria.

Little, A. and Smith, G. (1971): *Recherches sur les handicaps socioculturels de O à 7 ans*. Ministère de l'Education Nationale et de la culture française: Brussels.

Lopez Andrada, B. (1995) Necesidad de incidir en la detección precoz de alumnos potencialmente biendotados. *La orientación en el sistema educativo y en el mundo laborar*. VII Journadas de Orientación Escolar y Profesional. Madrid: AEOEP, pp. 276–80.

López López, E. (1990): 'La educación de niños desfavorecidos entre 0 y 3 años'. *Revista de Ciencias de la Educación*, No. 143, pp. 295–304.

Mainar, J. A. (1983) *Formación de conceptos: estrategias y niveles de asimilación de la realidad circundante al finalizar el preescolar.* Zaragoza: Instituto de Ciencias de la Educación.

Martin Moreno, Q. and Frontera Sancho, M. (1977) *La investigación en educación preescolar: trabajos de la red INCIE-ICEs.* Madrid: INCIE.

Mayer, R. S. (1971) A comparative analysis of preschool curriculum models. *As the Twig is Bent.* Boston: Houghton, Mifflin, pp. 286–314.

Miguel Diaz, M. D. (1979) *Diseño de un programa de educación compensatoria en función de los determinantes del rendimiento en el primer curso de EGB.* ICE, Universidad de Oviedo.

Ministry of Education and Science (1988/1996) *Documentos para la Reforma de la Enseñanza.* Madrid: MEC.

Peters, D. L., Neisworth, J. T. and Yawkey, T. D. (1985) *Early Childhood Education: From Theory to Practice.* Monterrey: Brooks/Cole.

Piaget, J. (1995) *El nacimiento de la inteligencia en el niño,* Madrid: Aguilar.

Pla Molins, M. (1995) *Expresión oral de conceptos científicos durante el segundo ciclo de educación infantil.* Unpublished Doctoral thesis. Madrid: CYGT.

Quintero, A. (1988) La innovación pedagógica en el programa experimental de educación infantil. *Enseñanza*, Vol. 6, pp. 9–27.

Rosenthal, R. and Jacobson, L. (1968): *Pygmalion in the Classroom: Teacher Expectation and Pupils' Intellectual Development.* Rinehart, Winston: New York.

Sierra, J. J. (1995) Metodo hipermedial de enseñanza para deficientes auditivos. *Estudios de investigación educativa en intervención psicopedagógica.* VII Seminario Nacional de Modelos de Investigación Educativa. Valencia: AIDIPE, pp. 110–11.

Stallings, J. A. and Stipck, D. (1986): Research on early childhood and elementary schools' teaching programs. *Handbook of Research on Teaching* McMillan: New York, pp. 727–53.

Stevens, J. H. and King, E. W. (1987) *Administración de programas de educación temprana y preescolar.* México: Trillas.

Taberner, C., Agote, A. and Aliaga, F. (1995) Centro comarcal de estimulación temprana: análisis de una experiencia. *Estudios de investigación educativa en intervención psicopedagógica.* VII Seminario Nacional de Modelos de Investigación Educativa. Valencia: AIDIPE, pp. 113–17.

Vecino, F. (1996) *Los aspectos métricos de la representación del espacio en los primeros años de la enseñanza.* Unpublished Doctoral thesis. Madrid: UNED.

Weikart, D. P. (1972): Relationships of curriculum teaching and learning, in Stanley, J. C. (ed.), *Preschool Programs for the Disadvantaged.* Johns Hopkins University Press, London.

Wiseman, W. (1964): *Education and Environment.* University Press, Manchester.

9

Positions in Swedish Child Pedagogical Research

Ulla Lind

What is threatening in the work of thinking (or writing) is not that it remains episodic but that it pretends to be complete.

(Jean-François Lyotard,1988)

Introduction

In this chapter I shall make an episodic and thereby somewhat biased account of research on preschool and childcare in Sweden. The aim is to give readers an orientation on research carried out in Sweden in recent years. This means that I do not survey and summarise all research which has been done. The examples of dissertations, projects and developmental work which I treat are chosen in order to represent directions and methodological perspectives which I wish to demonstrate. Each person has her limited viewpoint from which to observe and therefore I end the article by discussing my own context and the research approach with which I am most familiar. This also gives the reader the possibility of understanding the limits of the views I present.

Background

In Swedish childcare research, there has been a major developmental psychology perspective for many years. In comparison, however, it has still not been as prevalent in Sweden as in many other countries. When the State became involved during the 1960s and gave the field legitimacy, it also gave support to research which was connected to the governmental control system (Bergman, 1993). Thus Sweden lacks the use of strong 'child development' perspectives within research, which may have given the field legitimacy in other countries. The research was instead connected to governmental control and the implementation of the political decisions.

What is characteristic of this research is the presence of a number of questions which had already been formulated and to which the problematisation of the preschool field and childhood research was subordinate. Political scientist Bengtsson (1996) studies the implementation of the preschool reform of 1985–91. The reform implied preschool facilities for all children. The enquiry focuses on what government and parliament have been doing to reach their own policy goals. The implementation of government policies at local level was investigated through case studies of four local governments. The research highlights the large increase in the number of children in daycare centres during this period. But parliament failed to reach its goal and there appear to be no simple explanations as to why some local governments were more successful than others, in relation to local conditions (for a European comparison, see Kärrby, 1996).

Gunilla Dahlberg (1998) adds some thinking about the new political rationality supported by the metaphors of the market and the enterprise culture. She says that the preschool is seen as successful if it can promote *freedom of choice*, and proliferation and differentiation. Efficiency is increasingly related to the number of different profiles of preschools the local authorities can offer. 'Before the mid-eighties, very few preschools had leaflets on their programme. Today, many preschools have lavish leaflets of their programmes, and are producing exhibitions to explain and legitimise why their pedagogical approach should be chosen amongst other programmes available on the market' (Dahlberg, 1998).

Pedagogical and content questions had weak influence on Swedish research in the preschool field, until the late 1980s. Reduced economic resources and the State's new role after decentralisation caused evaluation and reflection to be expected to lead to greater problematisation of questions about efficiency and productivity in relation to new goals. As education and communication are seen as the strongest factors in a nation's image as a knowledge and information society, *pedagogical* questions about learning, knowledge and socialisation have become important to research, rather than *psychological* questions. Now the questions are more frequently of the type: 'What future approaches? What makes us think and act as we do? How shall we understand and participate in that which happens?'

Ten years ago research in this field presented a more unified picture. During the 1990s the picture has become considerably differentiated, including research using historical approaches as well as social science and curriculum theoretical perspectives which are connected to the socialisation process, political control, socio-linguistic and communicative processes. Further, a phenomenographic research perspective has developed which places the focus on learning, its content and cognitive processes.

Who researches child care?

Traditionally the area has been dominated by child psychologists, oriented towards cognitive and developmental psychology. During recent years the field has been augmented by the involvement of preschool pedagogues and teacher trainers (usually women) who have gained higher qualifications, so reaching research level. Discussion has also concerned the academisation of the preschool professions. It is a female-dominated area with low status, weak theory building and 'female' normative thinking with 'tacit knowledge', in which the re-creation of 'homely' private spheres is embedded. The preschools have rather been seen as complements to the home than as pedagogical environments for development and learning. Teachers become substitute mothers (Hultqvist, 1990; Tallberg Broman, 1991). According to Holmlund (1996), research on the supervision and upbringing of toddlers as a female profession has not interested researchers very much. The focus has, instead, been on the importance of childcare for working mothers. Hultqvist seeks to show that the history of childcare concerns the power of gender and thereby of the impotence of women.

That more women from childcare have begun to study the area is important from a methodological perspective, since it is likely that transitions away from a quantitative research paradigm are occurring as a result. The quantitative paradigm works chiefly through the use of large-scale questionnaire surveys and statistical analysis. Instead the attraction of more contextual perspectives has increased, with attempts to describe and deal thematically with the *complexity* which is typical of child pedagogical work. Above all, the researchers of today are interested in how *processes* in pedagogical practice appear and function. Pedagogical practices are thus studied not as *things* (objects) but as social practices. Preschool teachers who begin to undertake research themselves have a great interest in developing closer insights into the practice in which they previously worked, with the aim of creating more informed and detailed knowledge and understanding.

Maritha Lindahl (1996) describes a one-year-old's encounters with the preschool world:

As an active preschool teacher I was often fascinated by the youngest children's speculations and actions just at the beginning of their preschool stay. It thus felt natural to me to dedicate my work to an attempt to understand and illuminate the experience and learning of toddlers in this environment. (Lindahl, 1996, p. xiii)

Research context: facts and fundings

The Delegation for Social Research was reorganised in 1990 into an independent authority under the aegis of the Social Ministry: the Social Science Research Council (SFR). Its task is to promote and support basic and applied research within social science and social policy. Childhood and the family have been priority research areas.

Resources for special research positions were established in the 1990s with two professorships for childhood and family policy research, one at Linköping University in 'Childhood' and one at the Institute for Social Work in Göteborg. The first professorship in early childhood education and care was established at the Institute of Education in Stockholm in 1995. Another chair was created in 1997 at the University of Göteborg (Johanssson and Åstedt, 1996; Socialstyrelsen, 1997, p. 7).

A research survey from SFR (1996) on Swedish childhood and family research demonstrates the lively and multifaceted nature of this research area. Besides departments of pedagogics, psychology, sociology, political science, economics, social work, ethnology and cultural studies, departments also carry out research on children's conditions of life. The variety is also illustrated in a conference report from Socialtjänstforum in April 1997 – *Med fokus på barnen* (With a focus on children), a collaboration between the Swedish Municipal League, Central Union for Social Work and SFR.

The Swedish Council for Research in the Humanities and Social Sciences (HSFR) has engaged international scholars to review academic disciplines or research areas. The latest volume is *An Evaluation of Swedish Research in Education* (Achtenhagen *et al.*, 1997). In it they identify four 'blind spots', where there has been lack of discussion and research in Sweden: social and historical theory about postmodernity; social issues in the demography of schools; the reform-approach in the relationship between State planning and the normative function of research; and finally, strong critical comparative perspectives which would relate Sweden to international trends in education.

Childcare research – from equality to quality

Child care in Sweden was created to fill the double function of enabling parents (mothers) to work or study and to support and stimulate the child's development through pedagogical, directed activity at daycare centres. A riksdag decision from 1985 on 'preschool for all children' makes the municipalities responsible for supplying places for all children between 1 and 12 years of age whose parents work or study. In 1996 the responsibility for childcare was transferred to the Education Ministry. Education policy questions are now given a higher priority, following the Education Ministry's evaluation on extended schooling/out of hours care facilities *Grunden för livslångt lärande* (SOU, 1994, no. 45).

The National Board of Health and Welfare has published a pedagogical programme (curriculum document) for preschool services and it describes the basic pedagogical principles concerning childcare, for instance the central importance of play, the pedagogical content of care, creative development and the importance of relevant themes and pedagogy.

Since 1991 the National Board of Health and Welfare administers the majority of the governmental funds for local development work in childcare. The priority areas during recent years are local evaluation and (following changes in organisations and structures) quality work with special emphasis on: pedagogical work for younger preschool children; approaches for working with children who need special support; actions to develop alternative childcare; group-oriented and multicultural approaches; plus funds for building various networks for exchange of knowledge. Gunilla Roos (1994) certifies that most of the development projects carried on were strikingly similar all over the country, due to the fact that the government dictated the priorities.

No nationwide register of research and development work in childcare exists since the National Board of Health and Welfare's database (SOS-BAS) closed down in 1992. Universities and colleges provide information about their own initiatives and some centres have produced their own publications – for instance, the Centre for Knowledge about Children at Göteborg University, the Centre for Child and Youth Studies at the Institute of Education in Stockholm, the Centre for Childhood Studies at the University of Uppsala and the Centre for Child Culture Research at Stockholm University.

A new curriculum for children and youth

The research field covering childcare, preschool and school has intensified its activities and its focus following the latest school reform. After 1997 all six-year-olds will be admitted to the first class of primary school. A proposal for a new primary curriculum has recently appeared – *Växa i lärande* (SOU, 1997, no. 21) as well as a new curriculum proposal for the preschool *Att erövra omvärlden* (SOU, 1997, 157). These were preceded by a constant stream of evaluations and research on the quality of preschools, and about the differing traditions and historical origins of preschools and schools. (among others Dahlberg, Lundgren and Åsén, 1991; Dahlberg amd Åsén, 1991; Gunnesson *et al.*, 1992; Fredriksson, 1993; Dahlberg and Åsén, 1994; Morsing Berglund, 1994; Dahlberg and Lenz Taguchi, 1994; Fargo, 1995; Socialstyrelsen, 1995, 1995, no. 12; Andersson, Rohlin and Söderlund, 1996, no. 3; Pramling Samuelsson and Mauritzon, 1997).

In the curriculum texts, children are identified as individuals with different sexes, different cultural preferences, various ways of communicating, understanding and learning and with differing developmental projects to fulfil. This creates a number of important research questions in relation to the changing control rationale. From the State's point of view, there is a need for research to provide differential information and knowledge, whereas from the practitioner's point of view, contemporary pedagogical research seems to have become more a matter of tasks and identity, rather than a question of implementation.

When questions about the pedagogical content of learning and cognitive processes, communications, languages, culture and socially constructed meaning have been accentuated, even gender research gets increased emphasis. For example, Annerblom (1983) adopted a feminist perspective in discussions about changing gender roles in daycare, and Carlsson (1983) studied preschool children's conceptualisation of gender roles. Studies have been continually undertaken on the preschool as women's culture and explorations of preschool patterns in creating cultural and social sexual identities and the effects of different conditions on girls and boys (Qvarsell, 1991; Hägglund and Öhrn, 1992; Tallberg Broman, 1995; Hägglund, 1995; Holmlund, 1996; Odelfors, 1996; Lenz Taguchi, 1996; Birgerstam,1997; Ohrlander 1997).

Preschool settings have been studied, albeit insufficiently, in segregated residential areas, where many immigrant and minority ethnic families live. Some research projects have been carried out by ethnologists and social anthropologists (Ehn, 1986; Ronström, Runfors and Wahlström, 1995). They show that the ideals of equality and justice have led to an emphasis on similarity and homogeneity at the cost of plurality. That which is different has been toned down and, independently of differences, it is expected that all be integrated into a vision of 'Swedish'. In this symbolic construction the immigrant is always 'lacking' (as a Swede), which is above all constituted as a matter of mastering the Swedish language. In the preschools which were studied, Swedish language training has permeated pedagogical strategy in all everyday situations, ostensibly compensating for the 'lack' (of the Swedish language) and at the same time to provide an 'equal start' and the same school preparation as that of other children in Sweden. Since children in general are often seen as lacking, not yet adults (Näsman 1995), so children belonging to a mixed ethnic background will in many ways be considered to be doubly lacking. According to this analysis, some could even be seen as multiply lacking, as in the case of an immigrant girl with unemployed parents. More that one-tenth of all children in preschools in Sweden (about 43,000) have Swedish as an additional language. During the early 1990s half of these children had some form of home language support in childcare; today the proportion has decreased to 20 per cent (Socialstyrelsen, 1996). Intercultural competence in Swedish preschools is still found in small, unannounced and uncelebrated suburban islands and multicultural perspectives are practically nonexistent in teacher education and in research (Lundberg, 1991; Lahdenperä, 1997).

The methodological context: research approaches

I have chosen to mark off four research approaches and some of their key concepts. These approaches to some extent overlap each other in research practices and projects, but the division makes it easier to focus on methodological and ethical problems. The four areas are:

1. phenomenographic approach

2. ethnography

3. ethnomethodology and socio-linguistics

4. poststructuralism.

The three first approaches have been popular in Sweden for a long time. The post-structural perspective is as yet an infant just taking its first steps in this research field in Sweden. Internationally, poststructural feminist research practice has developed lively perspectives, which today also includes research on preschool and younger children.

It seems remarkable that a field such as childcare in Sweden has not adopted feminist theory of knowledge in its research to a greater extent. Traditional women's research (women's studies) has exhibited little interest in researching this area of child pedagogy. There are now signs that 'sex neutral' child pedagogy research can be deconstructed, to liberate new energy for this (low status) research field, populated as it is by children and women. In the Swedish context 'similarity' has dominated over 'difference' within equality policy and welfare policy in general. The high levels of representation of women in political assemblies, high numbers of employed women, statutory equality and generous economic family policy, has hidden the power of the gender system under a surface of equality.

The phenomenographic approach: research on representations and conceptions

Phenomenography goes back to German philosophy and theory of science, through Dilthey's (1833–1911) hermeneutics which developed into Husserl's (1859–1938) phenomenology and Heidegger's (1889–1976) hermeneutic phenomenology. This discourse is one of the stronger ties between the Swedish pedagogical field's philosophic and scientific bases and an inheritance from German romanticism, idealism, historicism, critical school and human sciences. It is from this tradition that the human science discourse comes, in which one talks about *understanding* spiritual life (the inner) and *explaining* nature (the outer) which belongs to the natural sciences. The human sciences attempt to re-create the thoughts of others and reconstruct the other's situation in order to re-live the other's spiritual life, representations, concepts, feelings, etc. *Understanding* is constructed in the process of the hermeneutic circle, in which the parts must always be understood in relation to the whole. Holistic understanding builds on knowledge about the different details. This is conceptually about the *organic* nature of the world, the way everything is connected. The concept of organism causes the individual consciousness always to come up short in the face of what is greater, the 'life' that one is part of is more inclusive than the conscious life. Modern organic figures of thought appear, for example, in the 'ecological' theories of social life and about the 'climate' in daycare centres and its significance for children's behaviour (Ekholm and Hedin, 1991).

Husserl sees *phenomenology* as an *unconditional* basis for all knowledge. It builds on seeing beyond all prejudice (pre-judgement) and theories about different phenomena, placing them inside parentheses, and substitutes a *reflexive* attitude, which gives a neutral, pure description of 'things in themselves' – as they show themselves and as we immediately experience them. Husserl's philosophy is even called an *experience philosophy*, and holds that the highest form of experience is through immediate presentation, that is 'presence'. It is important to distinguish between *how* objects are perceived, the *meaning* which is given to the experience and the *object itself*, its character.

This is recognisable in the starting points which the *phenomenographic* approach expresses. Marton (1981) distinguishes between the question *what something* is (first order perspective) and *how something is perceived to be* (second order perspective). The latter is identified as phenomenography.

The phenomenographic methodology has chiefly been used to study the content of *learning*. This perspective has been developed at the University of Gothenburg. In general phenomenography does not reveal what knowledge different persons have, but rather how they *perceive* something. The results express themselves not in relation to actual phenomena and how they are, but rather how differently they can be perceived by different persons. The perception is described as the *relation* between individuals and the outer world. It is a perspective which attempts to bridge or counterbalance the dualistic view of the inner subject and outer object. This line of thinking believes that the world is never what it appears to be. The basis of this research is a special method for interviews and their analysis. The interviews are semi-structured with some introductory questions that are common to all those being interviewed. Thereafter different themes are followed up which start from the answers of the individual person being interviewed. The difference between this and other techniques is that in analysing interviews the phenomenographic method does not aim at a general goal. The aim is to designate qualitative differences in the participants' conceptions and categorise these conceptions as they were expressed in the conversations.

Validity in phenomenography has been dealt with by emphasising the descriptive stance – being open for inspection and exploring other angles in analysing the data – in contrast to more theory-based research. Often more than one researcher will be involved, in order to confirm the identification of the categories in the concluding analysis, inter-researcher reliability being the goal. This has, however, been perceived by many more as a concession to the logical empirical and the positivist demand for objectivity. Another way of dealing with this problem is described in Johansson (1992) with 'To validate is to question' (according to Kvale). By describing both the realisation and analysis as carefully and clearly as possible, the results can be discussed and any mistakes by the researchers countered – for instance, if their own expectations have had too strong an influence on decisions about the categories. The results of phenomenographic investigations are presented as *category systems*.

Johansson (1992) interviewed teacher trainers using phenomenography, questioning them about their conceptions of traditions in the Swedish preschool and preschool teacher education. By tracing the traditions and the historical growth of the preschools back to the origins of Fröbel's pedagogics, social work and reform pedagogics, Johansson could show that childcare assumed the position of a relatively independent area as a professional education and research field.

Ingrid Pramling was appointed in 1995 to the first chair in early childhood education with a special emphasis on childcare didactics. As an example of an insider researcher, she has made investigations in close co-operation with preschool practitioners through interviews concerning preschool children's conceptions and thinking. Her dissertation from 1994 about *the basis of knowledge* tests a phenomenonographic approach in order to develop children's understanding of their environment. A subsequent study was done with the children when they began school (Pramling, Klerfelt and Williams Graneld, 1995). The focus in this study was how the transition from preschool to school functions for the children who during their preschooling participated in the earlier programme (to develop their understanding about their own learning/metacognition). The child's a priori manner of behaving towards its surrounding world is the basis for learning and changes how the child experiences that surrounding world. Pramling introduces the concept *development pedagogic* in order to indicate how this differs from traditional cognitive and developmental psychology. Focus is placed on the child's perception of different phenomena in the world as investigated. Pramling formulated a methodology for learning which positions itself between the preschool's psychological cognitive view and the school's formal subject-centred cognitive view.

Barbro Morsing Berglund (1994) also represents a phenomenographic research perspective in her dissertation about activities for six-year-olds in preschools. She has studied preschool programmes for six-year-olds, interviewed personnel and children, as well as observed environments, in relation to frame factors. Activities for six-year-olds are strongly marked by the heritage from Fröbel with thematically structured content. She argues that while the starting point should be the children's own fields of interest, there is a high degree of general, imposed themes about animals and nature, the changing of seasons, holidays, farm life and farm culture. Concepts from developmental psychology about children's *needs* and *maturity* have thoroughly dominated preschool teachers' ideas about appropriate activities for six-year-olds. An obvious example would be movement and play needs. Morsing Berglund points out that even the daily routines and terminology in the preschools still follow the style of planning from the early Fröbel-kindergartens. Terminology from that time is still in use and 'assembly' gathers the children in a circle on the floor.

Lena Rubinstein Reich (1993) investigated in her dissertation what happens during 'circle time'. She demonstrated that it is an activity which represents a time and meeting-place for community of friendship and solidarity as well as individual confirmation but at the same time it is a ritual for discipline with means of compulsion and sanctions.

Maritha Lindahl (1996) used video to document and analyse one-year-olds' encounters during their first weeks at daycare centres. Before the observations began the parents and children were visited in the home, where they told the researcher about the child's habits and experiences. Each child was filmed on many occasions, altogether about seven hours. In order to study experience and learning among toddlers, Lindahl interpreted characteristic patterns in the children's actions showing that every act has meaning from the child's point of view. The results show that learning occurs when a child arrives at a realisation. He or she develops from one way of apprehending something to a qualitatively different way of understanding it.

This study is an example of increasing interest in the youngest preschool children, inspired by recent infant research. The National Board of Health and Welfare and Pramling (1993) carried out a research survey *Barnomsorg för de yngsta* (Childcare for the youngest). The aim was to collect ongoing research information which would be useful in improving practice and to challenge and complement educators' experience-based knowledge.

Constructivism: a 'basic instinct' in pedagogics

Morsing Berglund (1994) points out that a constructivist approach is obvious in the preschool pedagogue's statements during interviews, but not in the concrete teaching situations with the six-year-olds. Instead, traditional methods similar to those in use in schools for older children limited the learning. Boel Henckel (1990) studied the relationships between representations and theories in practice and the way that preschool teachers translated words into deeds. Henckel showed that most of the teachers and those who intended to be preschool teachers saw the preschool simply as an institution for adaptability. Only a few looked upon preschools as places for development or compensation for disadvantaged home environments. Today this picture may have changed to some extent. Discussions and studies have displaced questions about language reflecting actions governed by thoughts. Instead enquiry tends to focus on situated learning, different knowledge-seeking strategies and processes.

Kihlström (1995) asked preschool teachers to describe what were significant roles for their profession. The results showed three perspectives: taking *care* of the children; *developing* the children's personal abilities and *teaching* the children certain subjects. Phenomenography often conflicts with a cognitive perspective with specified concepts about knowledge, as if a certain knowledge, already defined, exists 'out there' and which the child shall 'grasp'. This can be due to the ontological constructivist point of view in which the individual indeed creates his own meaning and understanding, by acting and interacting in the world, but ends up with knowledge as 'private property'.

From 'personality' to 'identity'

Today many social science researchers in Sweden work with social constructionism. This epistemological standpoint holds that we have no direct and abrupt access to the outside world. The only way to know about things is through one or another form of language, text and discourse. Different positions give differing access to language and forms of understanding. Concepts like 'situated cognition', 'lived experience', 'doing gender' accompany the socially constructed 'individual' who is discovered through different 'stories', narratives, language actions and communication systems. So 'personality' has been replaced by 'identity' and is somewhat changeable because we co-construct our identities depending upon varying positions. Different positions create limitations and possibilities for action and reflection in varying contexts and depend upon sex, race, class, age, occupation, etc. In ethnography processes and actions are in focus.

The ethnographic approach: research with participant field studies

Using this perspective, researchers attempt in different ways to come into close contact with daily life in preschools. They are present or themselves participants in the children's activities which are studied. They observe what is happening, ask questions, listen to what is said and collect all possible data which can illustrate the questions on which the study is focused. The researchers then examine the processes observed and search for relationships and creations of meaning which go on in the activities. From this perspective stems the concept 'grounded theory' through which researchers construct theory and concepts from the empirical data (by induction). Ethnography developed as a research approach in the 1970s, based on anthropology. The ethnographer's basic goal is to describe cultures and its personages who *construct* the social world both by interpretations of the world and by actions, which build on interpretations. Consequently persons, through their actions, build different social worlds and the aim is to improve understanding of how these worlds function.

Ethnographic preschool studies often combine different modes of data collections. This offers the possibility of testing validity of the conclusions from participant observation, varying types of interviews and conversations as well as analysis of documents, field-notes etc. Birgitta Odelfors (1996) investigated the conditions underlying girls' and boys' differing languages in making themselves seen and heard. An act of communication could be speaking, playing, moving, drawing or singing. Her aim was to identify the conditions which support or limit children in expressing themselves in communication in preschool. She labelled her field study *pedagogical ethnography*. The techniques used for data collection were observation, encompassing field-notes, video and interviews with the children. She focused on specific activities such as play, assembly, aged-related group activities and drawing. The results indicate that the adults contribute to the creation of space for the boys by responding more to them than to girls. The most central condition from the children's point of view is to be able to participate in play groups with peers. Even assembly seemed to be an area for promoting the boys rather than the girls – the boys were more able to use opportunities for verbal participation at assembly time. Odelfors uses Vygotsky's expression, that a zone of proximal development was created to a greater extent for the boys than for the girls. Additionally, there did not seem to be any difference between the ways in which female and male staff members behaved in this respect.

A case study by sociologist Karen Davies (1996) aimed to understand the social world, in this case caring, by combining phenomethnographic perspectives with attempts to discover the specific social relations and ideologies which underlie and determine or influence the thoughts and actions of individuals. Her study builds on five months of participant observation and forty interviews at two daycare centres. She describes her analysis as taking *double perspectives*, in a boundary zone between systems thinking and poststructuralism. This means attempts to understand and show what characterises caring and caring relationships at a more general level and which conditions influence caring. She also wants to show that the individual's actions are always bounded by context. This perspective makes visible both the variations inside the community of women and how women's subordination is connected with other hierarchies. Another concept which she uses is 'the rationality of caring'. Davies describes how, during participant observer fieldwork, she responded to the social relations and the role as an extra staff person to such a degree, that she increasingly gave up her researcher identity. By the final phase of the fieldwork she felt like a preschool teacher. Her reflections highlight an ethical dilemma in pedagogical ethnography – 'going native'. Such research methodology moves the researcher from the position of an invisible, objective translator of scientific discourse, into a subject among other responding subjects. With respondents as 'co-researchers' a process can evolve into collectively shaped 'emotional stress' – what previously was the researcher's own problems during fieldwork and after, now turns into joint burden and responsibility for all involved in the research .

Child interviews

Further examples of research with phenomenographic and ethnographic approaches show children increasingly placed in the foreground. This transition could be a reaction caused by many recent studies concerned with adults, pedagogues, principals and teachers, their conceptions, representations, actions and professional identity. Even parents' representations of childhood and childcare have been the subject of a dissertation (Persson, 1994). Since the relationship to the children is the pedagogue's working environment, their working conditions depend upon how and in what way they visualise, sense and understand children. Questions are raised about the children's own representations. How do things look from their perspective?

The child viewpoint is a concept that gives new direction to the traditional child-centred perspective. The importance lies in seeing children's special competencies as a point of departure for activities and childhood policy. 'Children's culture', meaning the children's own culture, has been explored since the 1970s, in Swedish child and school research (Qvarsell, 1991; Dencik, 1995a). Children as actors was also a theme in the Nordic Basun project, in which inclusive fieldwork and interviews were used to study the socialisation conditions of the modern child (Dahlberg, 1996; Dencik, 1995b; Kristjánsson, 1995).

The pedagogical programme for preschools (1987) uses the concept 'competence' to describe goals for the development of the children. Communicative competence and social competence reflect influences from sociology of knowledge discourses on the preschool curriculum theories from the 1980s. Socialisation research, curriculum theory and cultural theories have advanced in the 1990s with an emphasis on child perspectives, the exploring child, the voice of the child, and the child as co-constructor of a new meaning of citizenship for children that includes cultural freedom of expression. This can be seen as the background for frequent and traditional use of child interviews in child pedagogy research. Despite different methodological systems, they all have the child perspective in common (Hultqvist and Pettersson, 1995). Children were previously not considered reliable informants. Nowadays the child interview in research is very common. However, its expansion as a method does not stand in proportion to the theoretical interest that exists for it (Lindh-Munther, 1989). The dominance of developmental psychology perspectives on children has contributed to making the child's own views uninteresting or questionable according to Näsman (1995), since it portrays the child as not having sufficient knowledge, capacity or judgement to give an 'accurate' description of its situation.

Marie-Louise Hjort (1996) investigated children's thoughts about play in the preschool. Group interviews were conducted with preschool children, in combination with observations. Hjort maintains that despite an increase of research about the importance of play, many have not previously interested themselves in children's perspectives on play. Most play research has been conducted in the field of cognitive psychology, from adults' perspectives (see also Knutsdotter-Olofsson, 1996). Hjort's conversations with the children made it possible to interpret the intentions of the play actions in their contexts. Here the researcher did not start out from an abstract child who uses play in the same manner at all times. Hjort used a Polaroid camera to document the play and later used the photos to stimulate the child's memory and conversation in the interview situation. Her conceptual framework is located in a number of theoretical positions: cultural-history, and the ideas of Vygotsky, Bachtin, Leontjev and Elkonin.

Gunilla Lindqvist (1995) adopts a similar theoretical profile in a didactic study about play and culture in preschools. It is designed as a development project, in which Vygotsky's concepts of *mediated experience* and the dialectical process in the encounter between the culture (context) and the different play forms (the text) were the guiding precepts. She used video for documentation of play, regular observations and field-notes (diary), conversation with children and adults as well as documentary analysis (of activity reports). The usual description among play psychologists has been that the development of play goes in stages from play with objects, to symbolic play, to role play. However, another finding emerged from this study. Even the youngest children showed the capacity to interpret and give meaning through a sense for the situation and context. Lindqvist identifies two tendencies in the modern preschool debate which is even reflected in research. There are advocates of a *natural science* (scientific) model that builds on an 'abstract' child which in Piaget's terms lacks logical thinking and needs to develop this by intellectual challenges in order to be conscious about its thought process (exemplified by Pramling's (1994) development work). The other model, which Lindqvist calls *humanist*, is critical of rationally oriented pedagogy. She advocates a context-sensitive, narrative logic, according to a hermeneutical emphasis on interpretative processes. According to this view, even play needs to be re-evaluated, since play's attributes of change and transformation have importance for the processes of knowledge creation.

This research can be compared with two projects (Dahlberg and Lenz Taguchi, 1994; Lenz Taguchi, 1997) which discuss visions of the child, in which scientific rationality connects to a constructivistic view of learning. Transgressing conceptual polarities, these researchers formulated an approach which advocates that the child should be seen as co-constructor of culture, knowledge, identity and learning. Using deconstruction, they analyse power and the dominating discourses, which regard children as objects of knowledge traditions and prescribed pedagogy. This perspective has gained nourishment from a long-term exchange of knowledge and experiences involving inservice provision for preschool teachers in Sweden and the pedagogical philosophy in the municipal childcare of Reggio Emilia in Italy (Dahlberg and Åsén, 1997).

The ethnomethodological approach: research about everyday language, its function and meaning

Ethnomethodology means the study of the methods (methodology) used by the people (ethno) to produce and make sense of everyday life. In a closely limited meaning this research approach can be identified by conversation analysis, in which nothing except the speech should be drawn into analysis. *Speech action theory* draws attention to language as a human social *practice* and views language as *functional* rather than *descriptive*. Languages function to produce reality. Action (verbal and non-verbal) is embedded in a situation as it is created and in the *context* created by the conversation.

Traditional socio-linguistic studies view *context* as a number of background variables which are attributed to the individual participants; for instance, age, sex, social class and ethnicity. Language and discourses create reality and also create social order. Social order according to ethnomethodological thinking is thereby the *result* of the person's social actions and not a precondition for them.

Three dissertations from Linköping University, within the theme of childhood studies, represent research dealing with cultural production and cultural meaning creation among children. Marie Bendroth Karlsson (1996) has studied visual projects in preschools and the early school years. Her purpose has been to identify what projects develop into aesthetically cognitive processes and what do not. She demarcates a number of 'pedagogical dilemmas' in creative work with children. She used what she calls *micro-analyses* in order to analyse verbal and non-verbal interaction in art education activities which are documented by video camera. Karlsson attaches herself to the descriptive concept 'community of learners' (after Rogoff, 1994) in which the researcher assembles a picture of the ideal learning situation – the active child interacting with a guiding teacher, in a situation where everyone is learning.

Gunnlög Märak (1994) investigates children's ways of making meaning out of complex literary texts in her dissertation about children's interpretation of fictional characters´ thinking – 'On Snufkin's spring tune and a Bear of Very Little Brains'. She found that even preschoolers were able to talk about irony, metaphor and other underlying messages. One hundred and ten (110) children, from two communities took part in the study, for which Märak used semi-structured interviews after the children had listened to her reading a fairy tale. Central concepts in her analysis are *cultural capacity*, attached to age and socialisation environments, *taking perspective* and *cultural guiding*.

The children were guaranteed anonymity, the parents were informed by letter and the children themselves were required to give permission before participating.

In *Making Sense of TV-Narratives. Children's Readings of a Fairy Tale*, Ingegerd Rydin (1996) used interviews of 86 children in pairs, after they had seen a saga on TV. During the interview with one child, the other child drew pictures about the story. In order to provide a more multifaceted picture of children's readings of television, she analysed the child drawings. The patterns revealed in the interviews were confirmed by the drawings – the children avoided the setting almost completely, and focused on the episode of conflict introduction, the climax and resolution. The children appeared to choose those scenes from the story that were most important to them. The TV story was the 'raw' material, that the children used to fantasise over scenes of interest. Rydin uses the *tool kit* metaphor formulated by James Wertsch (with its origin in Vygotsky's tool concept). Rather than saying that a group 'possesses' certain ways of thinking, one should say that they have access to mental mediating tools and they choose the appropriate tools, depending on the context. Most importantly, forms of thinking acquired earlier are not substituted by more advanced forms of thinking as the individual grows older.

'Can different forms of knowledge also be non-hierarchical?' is a question posed by social constructionist perspectives. This is most challenging to the classical epistemological discourse, which has exalted rationalist thinking since the Enlightenment. Dealing with such a question demands theories about how power and control over discourses are produced. This leads on to another research approach currently influencing the social sciences and the question of the possibility of post-structural pedagogical research.

Post-structural research discourse: from introspection to reflection through deconstruction

When the researcher's study is considered as a *social and cultural construction*, instead of a vision of reality, self-reflection has been used as a tool for testing validity. Self-reflection is a clarification of what discourses and concepts have formed the researcher's thinking and actions. In this perspective deconstruction has a double function as analytic method, both to reveal the discourses and concepts that build up the structures that are researched, and to discover one's own thought structures.

Deconstruction is the post-structuralist way of investigating *how* discourses and texts operate in relation to each other. According to the deconstruction deriving from Derrida, we can analyse texts in particular areas, reveal the hidden contradictions and dichotomies (e.g. male/female, subject/object) and make the repressed meanings present for the reader. It is a methodology involving reading and describing without limit the number of *possible* interpretations. This is often described as giving different 'readings'. It aims at a *re-constructive* process by re-formulating, re-visioning, re-reading and *making choices* between multiple perspectives and various uncertainties. In deconstructive analysis, research is not at the level of the text, but at the level of the discourse. This activates the researcher's own subjective understanding. Deconstructive reading shows how we are led by the text into accepting the assumptions it contains.

Post-structuralism does not mean anti-structuralism. Rather it can be described as a philosophical and theoretical movement that tries to deal with postmodernism through investigations of discourses, social structure and social practices. Theoretical combinations of structuralism and post-structuralism can exist as a continuum, as a *dialogue* and as both. This means that contextualising provides the concepts to create different *stories* or *narratives*. This has also been described as 'the linguistic turn' or a transition from consciousness philosophy to language philosophy. Post-structural research is sometimes termed discourse analysis.

Post-structural theories centre on the 'text', rather on people/subjects and discourses. They show *how* identities are always produced through access to particular discourses. This follows from Foucault, who maintained that language cannot allow direct access to meaning. Knowledge, he held, is a form of discourse and language begins not with *expression*, but with discourse. From him we learn that discourse operates *as a form of power*, and that a discourse inscribes individuals/subjects as collectives.

Swedish researchers who have been inspired by Foucault often focus on historical material. Kenneth Hultqvist (1990) at the Stockholm Institute of Education investigated the preschool child, *Förskolebarnet*, as a construction of community and individual freedom. His analysis of the preschool discourse can be seen as a contribution to the history of the idea of the preschool child. The author gives perspectives on power and knowledge behind the image of the child as expressed in official investigations of the preschool.

Kajsa Ohrlander (1992) of the same institute has worked with analysis of discourse in an historical study entitled *I barnens och nationens intresse*. She studied social liberal reform politics from 1903 to 1930.

Her purpose was to draw attention to how a particular discourse – the 'winning' discourse – came to dominate speech and writing about preschool programmes, by locating the collective discourse that had existed *before* it had won.

Kerstin Holmlund (1996) focused on the struggle for childcare institutions in the period 1854–1968 in her study. She traced changes in two types of institutions and their personnel, from two professions. Her sources are archives, journals, investigations and protocols. Her theoretical concepts come from Bourdieu and his thought structures such as the concepts of social capital, habitus and field.

My neighbourhood: neopragmatic action research – from objectivity to 'solidarity'

Neopragmatic research analyses how language legitimates actions, by deconstructing discourses which claim to speak of how we should understand, discursive regimes and practices which dominate and have power over how we act. It builds on change, continuity, interactivity, reflective thinking and action. A relationship of solidarity must be maintained between the researchers and the teachers and children who are involved in the study, since according to the philosophy underpinning this approach, solidarity replaces the scientific requirement for objectivity.

By studying how discourses interact and by deconstructing the thinking which supports the dominating organisation of power, the researchers participate in ethical reflections over the knowledge which her/his research produces. The researcher deconstructs herself/himself at the same time that she/he supplies other instruments for scrutinising the basis of the power relations. The researcher must also strive to surpass the positions and identities which hinder the perspective of solidarity.

An example in my neighbourhood that I will label a neopragmatic, negotiated cultural project is a shared knowledge-seeking strategy of Swedish and Italian early child pedagogy and research. A continuous exchange has been going on for over twenty years through the work of the Reggio Emilia Institute in Stockholm and a research group at the Department of Child Studies at the Stockholm Institute of Education. The Reggio Emilia Institute was established in the early 1990s as a centre for continuous professional development for preschool teachers and other pedagogues. A recent step in this collaborative work is a four-year research and development project supervised by Gunilla Dahlberg and Gunnar Åsén from the

Stockholm Institute of Education. The project *Early Childhood Pedagogy in a Changing World*, financed by a grant from the Ministry of Social Affairs, involves thirty preschools in a district of Stockholm. They have worked with developing the content and methods of early childhood education through observation and documentation of pedagogical processes as instruments for change and learning. The project is oriented on praxis. It deepens questions about how pedagogical practices can constantly change and reshape content and the methods. Reggio Emilia's early childhood education can be described as a pedagogical approach based on ongoing narratives, a communicative process with artistic and creative projects capturing children's theories and fantasies, conversations, images, music, drama and all sorts of language games commenting on the children's contemporary social and cultural life as well as the historical and the natural environment. They work with subjects and questions that emerge from the concerns and interests of the children and develop creative learning processes with various tools, the arts, visual communication and pedagogical documentation. When you step inside a preschool in Reggio Emilia you can literally 'read' from the walls about the content. Visual diaries, photos, drawings, sketches, paintings and texts tell about projects.

The project *Early Childhood Pedagogy in a Changing World* has now evolved into a collective knowledge and identity project about sharing and learning organised in national networks for experience exchanges which brings together 35 local networks with schools and preschools all over Sweden, as well as a Scandinavian network with representatives from five countries. Symposiums and conferences are regularly arranged and publications are planned for 1998. Three doctoral students at the research department are researching at different preschools connected to the project. Hillevi Lenz Taguchi is investigating pedagogical documentation. She concludes that documentation is a practical tool for empowering children as well as teachers, who develop new constructions of knowledge about children, themselves and the learning process. Further, Taguchi claims it is crucial that children be given the freedom to construct their own ways of thinking and understanding in the early years (Lenz Taguchi, 1997).

The second research student, Elisabeth Nordin Hultman, is investigating the importance of the physical arrangements and the organisation of the 'pedagogical room' in preschools and schools. She is comparing pedagogical settings in England and Sweden. From videotapes and observations she reads the room and the objects as a 'text' that has been coded by various discourses, ideas and regimes about what should and should not happen in these milieus. The concepts and pedagogical ideas are seen as furnishing in much the same way as the objects and materials in the rooms. This can be described as analysing the 'grammar' of different pedagogical rooms. Her theoretical tools come from curriculum theories, semiotics and deconstruction.

My own research is a long-running ethnographic study of the youngest children in one preschool. I follow artistic learning processes and interpretations and conversations about video documentation of the children's work. Together with me, the preschool teachers work with interpretations of photos, videos and notes from observations.

Summary

In summary, Swedish research on preschool and childcare shows remarkable breadth and variation. It is stronger on questions of methodology than theory, but the theoretical developments which do exist are leading the way to new knowledge.

References

Andersson, B. E., Rohlin, M. and Söderlund, A. (1996, no. 3) *Skola – skolbarnomsorg i samverkan – Skolbom, Nr. 3.* Inst. för barn- och ungdomsvetenskap, Lärarhögskolan i Stockholm.

Andersson, G., Björnberg, U., Gustafsson, B. and Pramling, I. (1997) *Om svensk barn- och familjeforskning. En probleminventerande översikt.* Stockholm. Socialvetenskapliga forskningsrådet, 1996.

Annerblom, M. L. (1983) *Att förändra könsroller. Ett feministiskt perspektiv på diskussionen om könsroller på dagis.* Lund: CWK Gleerup.

Bendroth Karlsson, M. (1996) *Bildprojekt i förskola och skola. Estetisk verksamhet och pedagogiska dilemman.* Lindköping University, Institute of Tema Studies, Department of Child Studies.

Bengtsson, Hans (1996) *Förskolereformen. En studie i implementering av svensk välfärdspolitik 1985–1991.* Lund Political Studies 86.

Bergman, M. (1993) Early childhood care and education in Sweden, in Davies T. (ed.) *Educating our Youngest Children: European Perspectives.* London, Paul Chapman, pp. 113–32.

Birgerstam, P. (ed.) (1997) *Kvinnligt och manligt i förskolan.* Lund: Studentlitteratur.

Carlsson, M. (1983) *Sex-role opinions as conceptual schemata in 3–12 year old Swedish children.* Acta Universitatis Upsaliensis, 30.

Dahlberg, G. (1996) Negotiating modern childrearing and family life in Sweden, in J. Brannen and R. Edwards (eds.) *Perspectives on Parenting and Childhood: Looking Back and Moving Forward.* South Bank University of London.

Dahlberg, G. (in press) From the 'people's home' – *Folkhemmet* – to enterprise: reflections on the constitution and reconstitution of the field of early childhood pedagogy in Sweden, in T. Popkewitz (ed.) *Educational Knowledge: Changing Relationships between the State, Civil Society, and the Educational Community.* Albany N.Y.: The State University of New York Press.

Dahlberg, G. and Åsén, G. (1991) *Perspektiv på förskolan.* Stockholm: HLS Förlag.

Dahlberg, G. and Åsén, G. (1994) Evaluation and regulation: a question of empowerment, in P. Moss, and A. Pence, (eds.) *Valuing Quality in Early Childhood Services: New Approaches to Defining Quality.* London: Paul Chapman.

Dahlberg, G. and Åsén, G. (1997) Loris Malaguzzi och den pedagogiska filosofin i Reggio Emilia, in L. Svedberg, and M. Zaar, (eds.) *Boken om pedagogerna.* Stockholm: Liber Utbildning.

Dahlberg, G. and Lenz Taguchi, H. (1994) *Förskola och skola. Om två skilda traditioner och om visionen om en mötesplats.* Stockholm: HLS Förlag.

Dahlberg, G, Lundgren U. P. and Åsén, G. (1991) *Att utvärdera barnomsorg.* Stockholm: HLS Förlag.

Davies, K. (1996) *Önskningar och realiteter. Om flexibilitet, tyst kunskap och omsorgsrationalitet i barnomsorgen.* Stockholm: Carlssons.

Delegationen för Social Forskning (1989) *Barnomsorgen i ett samhällsperspektiv.* Stockholm: DSF och Socialdepartementet.

Dencik, L. (1995a) Välfärdens barn eller barns välfärd? Om till-syn, hän-syn och fel-syn, in K. Hultqvist, and K. Pettersson, (eds.) *Seendet och seendets villkor. En bok om barns och ungas välfärd.* Stockholm: HLS Förlag.

Dencik, L. (1995b) Modern family life in the Nordic countries, seen from the perspective of the child, in *Building Family Welfare.* Stockholm: Socialdepartementet.

Ehn, B. (1986) *Det otydliga kulturmötet. Om invandrare och svenskar på daghem.* Lund: Liber.

Ekholm, B. and Hedin, A. (1991) *Sitter det i väggarna. En beskrivning av daghemsklimat och barns beteende.* Linköping Studies in Education. Dissertation no. 32.

Fargo, L. (1995) *Barnomsorgens kvalitet.* Liber Utbildning.

Fredriksson, G. (1993) *Integration förskola, skola, fritidshem – utopi och verklighet.* Stockholm: HLS Förlag.

Gunnesson, M., Flising, B., Qvarsell, B. and Werner I–L. (1992) 'Samverkan för utveckling skola-barnomsorg'. Stockholm: Allmänna Förlaget.

Hägglund, S. (1993) Hurra det blev en pojke!, in *Visst är vi olika!* Från Arbetsgruppen Kvinnligt och Manligt i skolan, Utbildningsdepartementet, pp. 6–10.

Hägglund, S. and Öhrn, E. (1992) *Kön, utbildning och pro-social utveckling.* Inst. för pedagogik, Göteborgs Universitet. Rapport nr 1992:02.

Henckel, B. (1990) *Förskollärare i tanke och handling. En studie kring begreppen arbete, lek och inlärning.* Akademisk avhandling. Umeå: Pedagogiska institutionen.

Hjort, M. L. (1996) *Barns tankar om lek. En undersökning av hur barn uppfattar leken i förskolan.* Stockholm: Almqvist & Wiksell International.

Holmlund, K. (1996) *Låt barnen komma till oss. Förskollärarna och kampen om småbarnsinstitutionern 1854–1968.* Dissertation of the Faculty of Social Science, University of Umeå: Pedagogiska Institutionen.

Hultqvist, K. (1990) *Förskolebarnet. En konstruktion för gemenskapen och den individuella frigörelsen.* Stockholm: Symposion.

Hultqvist, K. and Pettersson, K. (eds.) (1995) *Seendet och seendets villkor. En bok om barns och ungas välfärd.* Stockholm: HLS Förlag.

Johansson, G. and Åstedt, I. B. (1993) *Förskolans utveckling – Fakta och funderingar.* Stockholm: HLS Förlag.

Johansson, J. E. (1992) *Metodikämnet i förskollärarutbildningen. Bidrag till traditionsbestämning.* Göteborg Studies in Educational Sciences. Acta Universitatis Gothoburgensis.

Kärrby, G. (1996) Sweden. in *A Review of Services for Young Children in the European Union 1990–1995.* Brussels: European Commission Network on Childcare.

Kihlström, S. (1995) *Att vara förskollärare. Om yrkets pedagogiska innebörder.* Göteborg: Acta Universitatis Gothoburgensis.

Knutsdotter-Olofsson, B. (1996) *De små mästarna.* Stockholm: HLS Förlag.

Kristjánsson, B. (1995) Varandets barndom – (be)varandets barnforskning, in K. Hultqvist and K. Pettersson (eds.) *Seendet och seendets villkor. En bok om barns och ungas välfärd.* Stockholm: HLS Förlag.

Lahdenperä, P. (1997) *Invandrarbakgrund eller skolsvårigheter. En textanalytisk studie av åtgärdsprogram för elever.* Stockholm: HLS Förlag.

Lenz Taguchi, H. (1996) The field of early childhood education pedagogy in Sweden. A female project of professionalization and emancipation? *Nordiske udkast. Journal for Critical Social Science,* Vol. 1, no. 24, pp. 41–55.

Lenz Taguchi, H. (1997) *Varför pedagogisk dokumentation?* Stockholm: HLS Förlag.

Lindahl, M. (1996) *Inlärning och erfarande. Ettåringars möte med förskolans värld.* Acta Universitatis Gothoburgensis.

Lindh-Munther, A. (ed.) (1989) *Barnintervju som forskningsmetod.* Uppsala, Uppsala universitet, Centrum för barnkunskap.

Lindqvist, G. (1995) *The Aesthetic of Play. A Didactic Study of Play and Culture in Preschools.* Acta Universitatis Upsaliensis. Stockholm: Almqvist & Wiksell.

Lundberg, P. (1991) *Utbildning och träning för interkulturell kommunikativ kompetens.* Lunds Universitet.

Lyotard, J. F. (1988) *Peregrinations. Law, Form, Event.* New York: Columbia University Press.

Märak, G. (1994) Barns tolkningar av fiktiva figurers tänkande. Om Snusmumrikena våvisa och en Björn med Mycket Liten Hjärna. Linköpings universitet.

Marton, F. (1981) Phenomenography – describing conceptions of the world around us. *Instructional Science,* Vol. 10, pp. 177–200.

Morsing Berglund, B. (1994) *Förskolans program för sexåringar*. Stockholm: Almqvist & Wiksell International.

Näsman, E. (1995) Vuxnas intresse av att se med barns ögon, in K. Hultqvist and K. Pettersson (eds.) *Seendet och seendets villkor. En bok om barns och ungas välfärd*. Stockholm: HLS Förlag.

Odelfors, B. (1996) *Att göra sig hörd och sedd. Om villkoren för flickors och pojkars kommunikation på daghem*. Pedagogiska Institutionen, Stockholms Universitet.

Ohlsson, J. (1996) *Kollektivt lärande. Lärande i arbetsgrupper inom barnomsorgen*. Stockholms Universitet, Pedagogiska Institutionen.

Ohrlander, K. (1992) I barnens och nationens intresse. Socialliberal reform-politik 1903–1930. *Studies of Psychology and Education* Nr. 39. Stockholm: Almqvist & Wiksell International.

Ohrlander, K. (1997) Matematik, längtan och flickor? *Locus*, Nr. 3/07 årg. 9, pp. 6–16.

Persson, S. (1994) *Föräldrars föreställningar om barn och barnomsorg*. Studia Psychologica et Pedagogica, Nr. 113. Stockholm: Almqvist & Wiksell International.

Pramling, I. (1993) *Barnomsorg för de yngsta – en forskningsöversikt*. Nya vägar inom barnomsorgen. Socialstyrelsen. CE Fritzes AB.

Pramling, I. (1994) *Kunnandets grunder. Prövning av ett fenomenografisk ansats till att utveckla barns sätt att uppfatta sin omvärld*. Göteborg Studies in Educational Sciences. Acta Universitatis Gothoburgensis.

Pramling, I. Klerfelt, A. and Williams Graneld, P. (1995) 'Först var det roligt, se´n blev det tråkigt och se´n vande man sig . . .' *Barns möte med skolans värld*. Göteborgs Universitet, Institutionen för Metodik i Lärarutbildningen, Rapport nr 9.

Pramling Samuelsson, I. and Mauritzon, U. (1997) *Att lära som sexåring*. Stockholm: Skolverket.

Qvarsell, B. (1991) Flickor och pojkars pedagogiska villkor. Om könsskill-nader i barnkulturen, in P. Kättström (ed.) *Flickor och pojkar. Om verkliga och overkliga skillnader*. Stockholms Universitet, Centrum för Barnkulturforskning.

Qvarsell, B. (1994) Tillbaka till Peirce? Tankar och begrepp kring den peda-gogiska etnografin. *Utvecklingspsykologiska Seminariet Skriftserie, Nr. 43*. Stockholms Universitet, Pedagogiska Institutionen.

Rogoff, B. (1994) Developing understanding of the idea of communities of learners, in *Mind, Culture and Activity*, Vol. 1, no. 4, pp. 209–29.

Ronström, O., Runfors, A. and Wahlström, K. (1995) 'Det här är svenskt dagis'. Et etnologisk studie av dagiskultur och kulturmöten i norra Botkyrka. Mångkulturellt Centrum, Botkyrka.

Roos, G. (1994) *Kommunerna och det pedagogiska utvecklingsarbetet. Omfattning och inriktning*. Acta Universitatis Upsaliensis No. 57, Uppsala Studies in Education.

Rosengren, K. E. and Öhngren, B. (1997) *An Evaluation of Swedish Research in Education*. Evaluation chapters by: Achtenhagen F., Bjerg J., Entwistle N.,

Popkewitz T., Vislie L. Historical chapter by: Härnqvist K., HSFR, Swedish Council for Research in the Humanities and Social Sciences. Uppsala, Swedish Science Press.

Rubinstein Reich, L. (1993) *Samling i förskolan*. Stockholm: Almqvist & Wiksell International.

Rydin, I. (1996) *Making Sense of TV-Narratives. Childrens Readings of a Fairy Tale*. Lindköping University, Institute of Tema Studies, Department of Child Studies.

Socialstyrelsen 1995:12 'Samverkan Skola-skolbarnomsorg'. En utvädering, Stockholm.

Socialstyrelsen (1996) Barnomsorg. Särtryck ur Socialstyrelsen (1996) Social service, vård och omsrog i Sverige.

Socialstyrelsen 1997:7, Statisktik Barnomsorg 1996 (Statistics – Social Welfare. Child Care 1996. Official Statistics of Sweden). Stockholm, Nordstedts AB.

SOU (1994) *Grunden för livslångt lärande – En barnmogen skola*. Stockholm: Utbildningsdepartementet.

SOU (1997) 21 *Växa i lärande. Förslag till läroplan för barn och unga 6-16 år.* Stockholm: Utbildningsdepartementet, Fritzes.

SOU (1997) 157 *Att erövra omvärlden. Förslag till läroplan för förskolan. Slutbetänkande av Barnomsorg och Skolakommittén.* Stockholm, Fritzes.

Tallberg Broman, I. (1991) När arbetet var lönen. En kvinnohistorisk studie av barnträdgårdsledarinnan som folkuppfostrare. Studia Psychologica et pedogogica, Nr. 99. Stockholm, Almqvist & Wiksell.

Tallberg Broman, I. (1995) *Perspektiv på förskolans historia*. Lund, Studentlitteratur.

Wiechel, A. (1993) *Fem förskollärares erfarenheter av sexårsverksamhet och syn på flexibel skolstart*. Malmö: Lärarhögskolan.

10

From Child Development to the Development of Early Education Research: the UK Scene

Tricia David

Introduction: looking back

Early childhood education research in the UK has, to an even greater extent than sectors relating to the education of older children, been dominated by child development research and the traditions of psychology. It must be acknowledged that we owe a debt to psychology and its 'relatives', such as psychoanalysis, for it is in part because of the emphasis on early childhood in the theories of Freud, Piaget, Bowlby and others that any consideration at all is given to what happens to young children. Despite the efforts of the early pioneers (e.g. Owen, Pestalozzi, Froebel, Montessori, McMillan and Isaacs, see David, 1990), nursery provision in this country was and remained neglected while other European states were setting up their near universal systems. Prior to the end of the 1960s there were very few textbooks for students of primary or early years education (Silver, 1985), so it seems hardly surprising that in the 1950s Piaget's theory was adopted by British teachers, creating a knock-on effect of assuming children under five to have certain limitations. Between the two world wars, Susan Isaacs (e.g. 1929) had been appointed to a post in child development at the London University Institute and her books formed the core of what was available for those training to work in the early years. What is still exciting about those books is the way in which Isaacs was challenging Piaget, with whom she corresponded. Sadly she died in the mid-1940s. Had she lived there might have been a more careful adoption of Piagetian assumptions during the 1950s and 1960s. Meanwhile, American developmental psychologists were dominating the world with ideas about children's supposedly universal developmental progression, irrespective of culture and society.

157

In 1965 an influential paper by Douglas and Ross (1965) was published claiming that children who had attended nursery provision gained cognitively and emotionally in the long run and with the publication of the Plowden Report (CACE, 1967) interest in early childhood grew because policy-makers were looking for 'best practice', attempting to measure effectiveness, in the hope that early 'inputs' would remedy any under-achievement caused by disadvantage. The policy-makers wanted returns on their investments. At that time UK policy and interest reflected that in the USA. Perhaps because both nations use English as their first language, the educational and education research ties have been strong. Similarly, the type of research which has been regarded as most desirable in both countries has generally been based on positivistic, natural science models.

Thus, when John and Elizabeth Newson (1965) carried out their innovative studies in which they adopted an interpretive paradigm, attempting to provide information about the lives of young children growing up in an urban society, co-constructing their worlds together with their families (still in the field of developmental psychology, of course), their work was regarded by some as lacking rigour.

In 1974 a review of current early childhood education research (Tizard, 1974) was published. Less than a third of those interviewed as part of the information gathering exercise were educationists, while a large proportion had backgrounds in psychology. The review had arisen in response to a government announcement of 1972 that nursery provision was to be substantially increased. Much research was commissioned to monitor that increase – although the plans to develop nursery provision never happened, supposedly because of a recession. Commenting that in most other European countries there had already been an expansion of services for young children, Barbara Tizard adds that the increases in provision had been mooted for two main reasons: firstly, the growing number of mothers wishing or needing to continue in employment outside the home (the 'care' reason) and secondly, the view that some children begin school at a disadvantage as a result of 'family variables' (Tizard, 1974, p. xi) and that an expansion of public provision would compensate for this, leading to higher levels of achievement at primary and secondary school. Her review categorised contemporary projects into the following research groupings:

- research concerned with the preschool; research with young children at home

- topics such as cognitive skills; evaluation of services; education and development of young children with severe learning difficulties

- social disadvantage

- other 'problems', such as early school socialisation, transition, general provision of services, staff training.

In her concluding remarks to this survey, which incidentally does not discuss research approaches, Tizard points out the inadequacy of research dissemination to practitioners at the time and the inadequacy of the nursery school model for parents who need more holistic services, integrating 'care' and 'education'. The persistence of these two themes over the intervening twenty years is an indictment of both policy-makers and those of us in the field!

The majority of the early childhood education research, like research into children's lives, consisted of large-scale studies. In 1972 a study by Davie, Butler and Goldstein was published, revealing the widening gulf during the school years between children born in poverty and those born into affluence. Much of the work of the National Children's Bureau, directed by Mia Kellmer Pringle, together with that of Jack Tizard at the Thomas Coram Research Unit, drew attention to the plight of children living in adversity.

Margaret Clark, who also conducted a survey of research evidence in the 1980s (Clark, 1988), points out that the economic and psychological ethos of the 1960s had not been conducive to the expansion of preschool provision, because of the shortage of teachers for older children and because of the powerful impact of findings about maternal deprivation (Clark, 1989). What was not challenged at the time was the fact that the findings about maternal deprivation were largely based on observations of children in situations which were severe and which could have been resolved through a more humane view of support for families, daycare and hospitalisation for children. Twenty-five years ago any expansion of public services was purely to cater for young children deemed disadvantaged and there were disagreements as to how best to teach them in order to remedy this situation. The emphasis in the early 1970s was still on what happened in the preschool setting, not what happened in the home, which was assumed. Many of the studies which were funded in the wake of the proposals to extend preschool provision in the UK seem to have been preoccupied with measurable variables such as the length of the day in the setting, the number of children in a group, the length of time in nursery and their effects on a child's progress as measured by intelligence tests. Other complicating factors in the UK include the variety of preschool provision, much of it relatively unregulated, and much of it seen as either social (e.g. playgroups – for the children's benefit mainly, although also to provide friendship and learning opportunities for parents) or socio-emotional (day nurseries – the public ones being for the 'rescue' of children whose families were in dire distress, or the private ones to cater for parents who worked; or childminders – again, for working parents). In other words, only the maintained (and some private) nursery schools and classes were seen as overtly educational in a cognitive as well as in other senses.

In one study begun in 1970 (Osborn and Milbank, 1987), some 13,135 children were traced and data collected about them at birth, at five years old and again at ten, when they were interviewed. The project provided the field with comparisons of children's achievements following attendance at different types of preschool provision, but as it relied on parental reporting about the type of preschool provision used, some question its soundness. However, it exemplifies the large-scale, positivistic methodology favoured at the time. It also raises questions about a key topic which has caused the development of two parallel traditions in both provision and research – the historical divide between 'education' and 'care'.

Yet on the whole this was an exciting era because so much research was funded and because researchers began to use what were called naturalistic observation techniques, research strategies derived from animal ethology. Examples include *Studies in Preschool Education* (Clark and Cheyne, 1979); the Oxford project (e.g. Sylva, Roy and Painter, 1980; Wood, McMahon and Cranstoun, 1980) and the Keele Preschool Project (Hutt *et al.*, 1989). Large numbers of children were observed in preschool settings and their behaviours logged in order to derive some 'laws' which could be generalised, about the effectiveness of preschool group provision. Since early language deficit was thought to be in large part responsible for later school failure, this too was the focus of a number of large-scale studies (for example Clark and Cheyne's 1979 study included this element). Other research on language development and reading from within the UK (e.g. Clark, 1976; Tough, 1976; Wells, 1986) and from abroad (Clay, 1972) was widely discussed by early years professionals.

The technique of non-participant observation, requiring the researcher to be 'a fly on the wall', was also used in home settings by Davie *et al.* (1984) – the 'sister' team to the Keele project mentioned above. Another 'home' study by Tizard and Hughes (1984) was important in that it challenged earlier assumptions about the lack of stimulation in working class homes.

Meanwhile, in a somewhat different research tradition, coming from a more sociological perspective, Brian Jackson's (1979) *Starting*

School provided a rich collection of case studies of children's lives in a disadvantaged area in the north of England, during the period just before and during their admission to primary school. This type of lyrical, thickly descriptive study provided the field with research which was wholly meaningful to practitioners, moving emotionally as well as being intellectually challenging. Subsequent studies in a similar vein are Hilary Minns's *Read It to Me Now!* (Minns, 1990) and Carol Fox's *On the Very Edge of the Forest* (Fox, 1996). These are deep, fine-grained studies of the experiences of a small number of children. They are attempts to tease out the meanings co-constructed by the children and those who share their lives. In a similar way Carolyn Steedman's (1982) *The Tidy House* sought to expose the ways in which young girls try to make sense of and deal with the gendered nature of life for the women in their families and the women they know they will become. Perhaps one of the most recent studies to focus on the lives of a small group of young children is that of Andrew Pollard (Pollard with Filer, 1996). Here he traces the school experiences of five children between the ages of four and seven in an ethnographic study which provides evidence of the impact of children's social relationships and sense of identity on their approaches to learning.

To this day, it is probably true to say that developmental psychology holds a greater sway over early childhood research than any other discipline, although it is now recognised that a widening, multi-disciplinary approach to understanding the field is vital. The largest project currently under way is led by Kathy Sylva, begun when she was Professor of Child Development and Primary Education at the London University Institute of Education. This project continues in the tradition of searching for the characteristics of the most effective preschool provision. In addition, Emeritus Professor Colwyn Trevarthen's work (e.g. 1992), though neuro-physiological rather than psychological, is highly regarded for the support it gives to theories about the need for interaction and meaning-making in early childhood.

Who does early childhood education research in the UK?

While the history of early years education research lies mainly in the field of developmental psychology, this is not so today. Like other educational research, the majority is carried out by tutors in higher education (universities and colleges), and by researchers at specialist units such as the National Children's Bureau's Early Childhood Units

(London and Wales), the Thomas Coram Research Unit of the London Institute, the National Foundation for Educational Research and the Scottish Council for Educational Research.

Two studies which stand out historically as having been carried out by practitioners (or ex-practitioners) of education rather than by psychologists or academics are Parry and Archer's (1974) *Pre-school Education*, which was funded by the Schools Council, and a small survey of nursery provision for children with special educational needs, undertaken by HMI, following the 1981 Act (DES, 1982). Only rarely did practitioners in the past engage in research themselves, except for a few completing higher degree theses. Over the last twenty years the number of early years teachers undertaking research has increased, not simply as a result of the slow momentum towards the recognition that early childhood is a subject for serious study, but also because more universities have become involved in training early years teachers and because different kinds of evidence about early learning has been required (e.g. Cleave and Brown, 1991; Sharp, 1997; Tymms, 1997), as the scene in nursery and primary education has changed, with children now entering formal school at only four years of age in most parts of the country.

Paradigms, methods and influences

As I have already explained, the research tradition derived from the natural sciences and positivism has dominated research in early childhood education. However, more recently, a number of large-scale as well as many small-scale projects (both for higher degree dissertations and theses and as part of education tutors' and teachers' own work) have begun to adopt other paradigms. To begin with, the divide was seen as between quantitative and qualitative work, but nowadays it is recognised that both can be put to good use. It is more a question of what is done with the results, how participants are viewed and treated and the definitions of rigour, validity and reliability adopted. A good example of this is the funded, large-scale *Effective Early Learning* project, led by Professor Christine Pascal at Worcester College (Pascal *et al.*, 1995). The project aims to engage closely with those involved in preschool settings, so deriving largely qualitative, though with some quantitative, data which are illuminative and are used in an action-research model. Similarly, the *Principles into Practice* project based at Goldsmiths College (Blenkin *et al.*, 1998) adopted an action-research model and the practitioners engaged in continuing professional development through their own action-research projects.

More projects are beginning to use ethnographic techniques, to enter into the meanings shared by the adults and children in a particular setting in a particular place at a particular time (e.g. David Hartley's study of three nurseries in Scotland, 1993). The interpretive paradigm is developing apace, along with narrative approaches. But feminist, critical and postmodern underpinnings are at present less in evidence, although they too are increasingly used in this field.

Concepts, assumptions, ethics and values

Debate about reflexivity and the ways in which research is affected by the researcher's own cultural background and assumptions is really only just beginning in early years research circles in the UK. And while ethical considerations have long been part of medical research, ethics committees to consider projects involving young children in preschool settings are just beginning to exist. Similarly, children's wishes to be involved in the research process (or not) are now more likely to be regarded as a question researchers must consider, rather than simply relying on the permission of teachers, carers and parents, as in the past.

Connected with this, of course, is the question about the research paradigm adopted, and the view of human life, of whose world is being reflected upon by the research. Examples such as King (1978) in which the researcher did not consider the young children in whose classrooms he was observing capable of responding to any questions he might have, tell us much about the 'objectivity' of research carried out by people who are not well known to the children and who do not know them. As Deloache and Brown (1987) have pointed out, much research carried out in the past treated young children as deficient, rather than exploring the ways in which the research model might be deficient.

Links with theory

Athey's (1990) project involving parents and preschool staff in sharing observations of young children's schemas and Corinne Hutt's work on play (Hutt *et al.*, 1989) are examples of research based on Piagetian theory. More recently, there are examples which base their work on Vygotskyian perspectives, such as Bennett, Wood and Rogers' (1997) study, built on the narrative research paradigm to gain important insights into teachers' understandings and use of play with young children. Cochran's international team (Cochran *et al.*, 1990) included a researcher in Wales, and this was one of the few projects to have adopted Bronfenbrenner's (1979) ecological model of human development as its theoretical underpinning. And in fact, although exciting work is being done in the UK by groups interested in the sociology of childhood (see, for example, James and Prout, 1997), only a very small band of early years researchers have begun to adopt theory concerning constructions of childhood, begun by William Kessen in the late 1970s (Kessen, 1975; 1979), as their conceptual framework.

Commissions and omissions

Early years practitioners carrying out small-scale projects have continued to focus on play and learning, so too have some teacher trainer researchers (e.g. Bennett, Wood and Rogers, 1997), or professional aspects which take this into account (e.g. Abbott and Moylett, 1997; Blenkin *et al.*, 1998). However, it seems likely that early years education research will be forced more and more to focus on aspects of the education agenda creating a pressure for changes in practice due to developments in primary schooling. The implementation of the National Curriculum was found to have had a downward pressure on nursery education (Sylva, Siraj-Blatchford and Johnson, 1992). The advent of the New Labour government has created an urgency to ensure nursery places exist for all four-year-olds and soon the same will be true for all three-year-olds whose parents seek a place (though as yet funding is only available for part-time provision). The expansion of care facilities for younger children is an intention and the integration of care and education for all children in this age group is high on the list of priorities. Meanwhile, the government has initiated its strategy for tackling under-achievement in literacy and numeracy through special 'hours', with pre-set teaching plans, dedicated to these areas of the curriculum. The literacy and numeracy strategies include the first classes of the primary school, where most four-year-olds are found. At the same time, baseline assessment data (tests of children's language and literacy, numeracy, and personal and social development) are being collected at the start of their primary school careers, partly as a diagnostic tool and partly to assess each school's 'value added score' – supposedly as a measure of the school's effectiveness in educating the children between entry and age seven. Research and evaluation of these measures will be vital. Similarly, the effects of new teacher training requirements (DfEE, 1997) demand careful research attention. As Halpin and Troyna (1996) point out, research can be either a way of checking or validating a system (providing merely ideas for 'tinkering') or a challenge to that system. Foci such as equal opportunities relating to special educational needs, 'race', bilingualism and gender, which were important during the 1980s and early 1990s must not be lost.

The Teacher Training Agency (TTA), which has the responsibility of ensuring sufficient teachers are trained to appropriate levels to take up posts, including headships, within schools, provides small amounts of funding for teachers to conduct research in their classrooms and schools, with the hope that their work can be disseminated widely among colleagues and to support the TTA intention that teaching be a research-based profession. Like all early years research at this time, TTA-funded projects run the risk of being dominated by work within a very narrow, school and literacy range. Some educationists, not only in the early years sector, fear that an over-emphasis on narrow core skills is leaving too much of children's emotional learning, in particular, to chance (McCarthy, 1998) and recent projects point to the importance of self-esteem in young children's learning (Roberts, 1995). Another strand now deemed very important by policy-makers is cost-effectiveness, and the Audit Commission and the National Children's Bureau have carried out research relating to this aspect of nursery provision.

The dissemination and uses of early childhood research

Publishing early years research

Many early years education researchers publish their findings in books and journals, of which there are 146 academic and 101 professional education journals (LISE, 1997). However, in the main they publish in the five refereed, specialist academic early years journals currently edited in the UK, plus a small number of practice-based journals, such as *Child Education* and *Nursery World*, both of which include research information and research-based discussions of practice. Articles in the latter type of journal would not have been expected to count towards an academic's submission to a Research

---

[1] Research Assessment Exercises are carried out by the Higher Education Funding Council in order to decide on financial allocations to universities and colleges on the basis of their performance in research.

Assessment Exercise (RAE)[1] in the past, despite their potential for impact on practice. (*Child Education* has a monthly circulation in excess of 75,000 copies.)

Conferences and seminars

Organisations such as the European Early Childhood Education Research Association (EECERA) and British Educational Research Association (BERA) encourage the dissemination of research through conferences as well as through their related journals. BERA also encourages the formation of special interest groups (SIGs) and it is hoped that an Early Years SIG will spring to life at the BERA annual conference of 1998 in Belfast, initiated by Angela Anning (Professor of Early Childhood Education at Leeds University) and myself, although foundational work by Pat Broadhead (1996) and Cathy Nutbrown and Iram Siraj-Blatchford (who organised symposia) must be acknowledged.

It is difficult to assess the extent to which research impacts on the field. Studies such as that by Shirley Cleave and Sandra Brown (1991) about four-year-olds in primary schools provided a wealth of information but still one sees children's time being wasted in certain inappropriate practices. On the other hand, it is possible that many schools have heeded this research and have developed early childhood units, bringing the nursery and reception classes closer together. It is certainly the case that Stephen Tyler's (1979) research which culminated in the *Keele Preschool Assessment Guide* has had a long-lasting influence on ideas about assessment and record-keeping in nurseries, since his model is visible in those produced by local authorities and individual schools over the two decades.

Funding issues

Competition for funding for research has become stronger in the last ten years. The main funding bodies for early years education researchers working in universities and colleges of higher education are the ESRC (Economic and Social Research Council), the Nuffield and the Leverhulme Foundations and the Esmée Fairbairn Foundation. The Department for Education and Employment (DfEE) also funds some research (e.g. the current early years education project mentioned above headed by Kathy Sylva). However, the majority of projects by small teams in higher education and those carried out in conjunction with practitioners are usually funded by local authorities or by the universities, or by individuals themselves.

Other organisations which occasionally either undertake or commission research include the teachers unions and, for example, OMEP UK (World Organisation for Early Childhood Education, UK Committee) or BAECE (the British Association for Early Childhood Education).

International influences and collaboration

Firstly, the fact that researchers and practitioners in the UK use English as their first (and often only) language has meant that, on the one hand, they have relatively easy access to research reports and discussions from North America and Australasia, and on the other hand, unless work is available in translation, only a few have been able to truly enter into dialogue with the work of European colleagues. So, for example, the study of *Childhood in Three Cultures* (Tobin, Wu and Davidson, 1989), or Barrie Thorne's (1993) work on gender, Jill Rodd's on leadership (1994), or Vi McLean's (1991) *The Human Encounter*, and High/Scope papers (e.g. Schweinhart and Weikart, 1993) have become key texts for early childhood education research courses, for their methodologies as much as for substantive issues. Research reports of colleagues who speak and write in other languages have been made increasingly available through the growing number of international journals, networks and conferences and especially as a result of the work of Peter Moss and the European Child Care Network (see Helen Penn, Chapter 2) and subsequent publications which have arisen from this group. It is interesting that during the time these publications have been emerging the care/education divide in the UK seems to have narrowed, with collaborations between those from a strongly 'education' background and the protagonists (historically) of 'care' developments in the interests of working mothers. As a result of both practitioner and researcher interest in the nurseries of Reggio Emilia, there has been greater recognition for the support and challenge researchers from the two ('education/care') traditions can give to each other. The international perspectives offered in publications such as *Valuing Quality in Early Childhood Services* (Moss and Pence, 1994) and those emerging from the work of the European Child Care Network have helped move the debate about integrated services on from the UK's earlier care/education arguments.

The ways in which international interaction and collaborative research networks challenge national or regional assumptions have also had an impact on the early years research community in the UK. The growth in the number of projects like *Childhood as a Social*

Phenomenon reported and commented on by its participants in *Childhood Matters* (Qvortrup *et al.*, 1994), which draw attention to the assumptions made by those in power and their influence on the ways in which members of that society, including the researchers, think about young children, is to be welcomed. They also act as a brake on the export of culturally inappropriate curricula and constructions of childhood to the majority world, as sensitivity to this 'curricular imperialism' improves. Similarly they should signal the danger in adopting wholesale the ideas, policies and teaching methods of other, seemingly successful countries. Gunilla Dahlberg tells a powerful story about the late Loris Malaguzzi, key philosopher and teacher in the development of the world-renowned nursery provision of the Emilia region in northern Italy, which is currently having a tremendous influence on both researcher and practitioner thinking in the UK. Some time after a group of Swedish educators had visited the Italian nurseries, Gunilla returned and Malaguzzi asked her how the project was advancing. 'Are there lots of "the dove"?' he asked, meaning thematic work around 'the dove', which was the theme the educators had seen during their visit. Gunilla admitted there had been and that this meant the Swedish group had not only adopted simply the surface meaning of the Reggio Emilia provision at this point, they had failed to centre their work on what was relevant to the lives and immediate interests of Swedish children.

Conclusion: future challenges

It has not been possible in a chapter of this length to do credit to the full range of work being conducted by researchers in early childhood education in the UK. In particular, I recognise that the chapter pays insufficient attention to research into the education and early identification of children with special needs – and in some senses this has become a specialist field in itself.

As with other aspects of work in the field of early childhood, the status of early childhood education researchers, largely women, is not high. To what extent this is due to gender, historical factors and the sometimes macho culture of education research circles or to our own rather inward-looking culture (signalled by the low rate of applications for ESRC research grants for early years projects, infrequent publishing in general education journals, etc.) one cannot say. Perhaps the situation is even more complex than this. We could begin to remedy the position of early years research, however, through developing local research groups based on collaboration between neighbouring universities and colleges together with local teachers' networks; mentoring younger/newer colleagues in the field; encouraging wider publication and dissemination of research findings.

Reading research specialists in the UK (e.g. Hall, 1987; Nutbrown and Hannon, 1997) recognise that there is much enjoyable activity to share with young children before they are expected to engage in formal literacy and it is interesting to note in this volume that Broström and Vilien tell of increasing research interest in early literacy in Denmark (Chapter 3). A survey of the evidence on language development, research and the early years curriculum (Mills, 1998) warns against early over-formalisation, citing Hungary, Switzerland and Belgium as countries with children whose later literacy scores are generally high and who are not expected to be readers in a formal sense until they enter primary school at at least six years old. It seems reading research will be high on the European agenda for some time, hopefully not simply about tinkering with existing policy and practice.

At the time of writing (spring 1998) there is some deep questioning of educational research generally, with the Chief Inspector of Schools commissioning a researcher to investigate the foci of work reported in four 'elite' academic journals, largely as an element in discussions about the relevance, or otherwise, of educational research. A second review, by the Institute for Employment Studies and commissioned by the DfEE, asks those in the field to respond to a number of questions, such as what constitutes research and does the right balance exist between different forms? This project also asks about the research process; review and evaluation; dissemination; and implementation. Professor Michael Barber, adviser to the government on standards in education, is said to have indicated that educational research is going to change appreciably. Whether this means a move away from reflective (critical or analytical research) to more empirical or creative research (inventing new systems), or whether researchers' ability to challenge government edicts will be limited by future policy changes, remains to be seen. As the submission to this project from the British Educational Research Association (forthcoming) points out, all types of research are vital in a democracy.

The maintenance and development of greater international links in early years research may prove both a safeguard and a catalyst in seeking to understand our own societies and their expectations of young children. Europe as a community of nations has exciting possibilities in many areas of life, but we must be aware that Western/Northern models of early childhood generate similar societal expectations, with the concomitant limits this may put on future generations. Perhaps what research demonstrates above all is that early childhood is constructed by its society, according to the needs and position of that social group. Sally Lubeck (1986) showed this to be true in her qualitative study of two preschool groups in two very different neighbourhoods in an American city. The young children in one were learning to be competitive individualists, while in the other they were learning to be co-operative group members. What we really need is for children to grow with the capacity to be both interdependent and co-operative as well as brave individuals. What we can learn from research in other countries, once the ideologies underpinning the research assumptions are problematised, is what can challenge us most. For example, soon after the Berlin Wall fell in 1989, some Eastern European and Western European early childhood researchers and practitioners were exploring the idea of democracy in relation to the education of young children. 'You will have to teach us all you know,' said the Eastern European seminar members. 'But maybe you know more about membership of groups, of society, about working together,' said a Western delegate, 'maybe all we know about is individualism and the young child.'

In a similar way, a Nigerian colleague invited me to visit her, adding that in her country they really know how to live with young children, many adults sharing the joys and the effort of child-rearing in the compounds. Research which began to show that we, in the UK, have some notion of what is meant by the African proverb 'It takes a village to raise a child' would certainly be progress.

References

Abbott, L. and Moylett, H. (eds.) (1997) *Working with the Under-3s.* Buckingham: Open University Press.

Athey, C. (1990) *Extending Thought in Young Children.* London: Paul Chapman.

Bassey, M. (1994) Educational research in the United Kingdom, in J. Calderhead (ed.) *Educational Research in Europe.* Clevedon: BERA/Multilingual Matters.

Bennett, N., Wood, L. and Rogers, S. (1997) *Teaching through Play.* Buckingham: Open University Press.

BERA (forthcoming) Submission to the DfEE project on Educational Research.

Blenkin, G., Kelly, V. *et al.* (1998) *Principles into Practice.* London: Paul Chapman.

Broadhead, P. (ed.) (1996) *Researching the Early Years Continuum.* Clevedon: BERA/Multilingual Matters.

Bronfenbrenner, U. (1979) *The Ecology of Human Development.* Cambridge

Mass: Harvard University Press.

CACE (1967) *Children and their Primary Schools.* (Plowden Report). London: HMSO.

Clark, M. M. (1976) *Young Fluent Readers.* London: Heinemann Educational.

Clark, M. M. (1988) *Children Under Five: Educational Research and Evidence.* London: Gordon and Breach.

Clark, M. M. (1989) *Understanding Research in Early Education.* London: Gordon and Breach.

Clark, M. M. and Cheyne, W. M. (eds.) (1979) *Studies in Preschool Education.* London: Hodder and Stoughton-SCRE.

Clay, M. M. (1972) *Reading: the Patterning of Complex Behaviour.* Aukland: Heinemann Educational.

Cleave, S. and Brown, S. (1991) *Early to School.* Slough: NFER-Nelson.

Cochran, M., Larner, M., Riley, D., Gunnarsson, L. and Henderson Jr, C. R. (1990) *Extending Families.* Cambridge University Press.

David, T. (1990) *Under Five – Under-Educated?* Milton Keynes: Open University Press.

Davie, R., Butler, N. and Goldstein, H. (1972) *From Birth to Seven.* Windsor: NFER-Nelson.

Davie, C., Hutt, S. J., Vincent, E. and Mason, M. (1984) *The Young Child at Home.* Windsor: NFER-Nelson.

Deloache, J. S. and Brown, A. L. (1987) The early emergence of planning skills in young children, in J. Bruner and H. Haste (eds.) *Making Sense.* London: Methuen.

DES (1982) *Children with Special Needs in Nursery Schools.* London: HMSO.

DfEE (1997) *Circular 10/97.* London: The Stationery Office.

Douglas, J. W. B. and Ross, J. M. (1965) The later educational progress and emotional adjustment of children who went to nursery schools or classes. *Educational Research* Vol. 7, no. 2, pp. 73–80.

Fox, C. (1996) *On the Very Edge of the Forest.* London: Cassell.

Hall, N. (1987) *The Emergence of Literacy.* Sevenoaks: Hodder and Stoughton.

Halpin, D. and Troyna, B. (eds) (1996) *Researching Education Policy: Ethical and Methodological Issues.* London: Falmer Press.

Hartley, D. (1993) *Understanding the Nursery School: a Sociological Analysis.* London: Cassell.

Hutt, S. J., Tyler, S., Hutt, C. and Christopherson, H. (1989) *Play, Learning and Exploration.* London: Routledge.

Isaacs, S. (1929) *The Nursery Years.* London: RKP.

Jackson, B. (1979) *Starting School.* London: Croom Helm.

Kessen, W. (1975) *Childhood in China.* London: Yale University Press.

Kessen, W. (1979) The American child and other cultural inventions. *American Psychologist,* Vol. 34, no. 10, pp. 815–20.

King, R. (1978) *All Things Bright and Beautiful?* Chichester: Wiley.

LISE (Librarians of Institutes and Schools of Education) (1997) *Guide to British Educational Journals.* London: LISE.

Lubeck, S. (1986) *Sandbox Society.* Hove: Falmer.

McCarthy, K. (1998) *Learning by Heart*. London: Gulbenkian Foundation.

McLean, S.V. (1991) *The Human Encounter*. London: Falmer Press.

Mills, C. (1998) *Britain's Early Years Disaster*. Paper on research survey conducted for the Channel 4 television documentary *Too Much Too Soon*. London.

Minns, H. (1990) *Read It to Me Now!* London: Virago.

Moss, P. and Pence, A. (eds.) (1994) *Valuing Quality in Early Childhood Services*. London: Paul Chapman.

Newson, J. and Newson, E. (1965) *Patterns of Infant Care*. Harmondsworth: Penguin.

Nutbrown, C. and Hannon, P. (1997) *Preparing for Early Literacy with Parents*. Nottingham: NES Arnold.

Osborn, A. F. and Milbank, J. E. (1987) *The Effects of Early Education*. Oxford: Clarendon Press.

Parry, M. and Archer, H. (1974) *Pre-school Education*. London: Schools Council-Macmillan Educational.

Pascal, C., Bertram, A., Ramsden, F., Georgeson, J., Saunders, M. and Mould, C. (1995) *Effective Early Learning Research Project*. Worcester: Worcester College of HE–Amber Publishing Co.

Pollard, A. with Filer, A. (1996) *The Social World of Children's Learning*. London: Cassell.

Prout, A. and James, A. (1997) *Constructing and Reconstructing Childhood* (2nd edition). London: Falmer Press.

Qvortrup, J., Bardy, M., Sgritta, G. and Wintersberger, H. (eds.) (1994) *Childhood Matters*. Aldershot: Avebury.

Roberts, R. (1995) *Self-Esteem and Successful Early Learning*. London: Hodder and Stoughton.

Rodd, J. (1994) *Leadership in Early Childhood*. Buckingham: Open University Press.

Schweinhart, L. J. and Weikart, D. (1993) *A Summary of Significant Benefits: the High/Scope Perry Preschool Study Through Age 27*. Ypsilante: High/Scope Press.

Sharp, C. and Hutchinson, D. (1997) How do season of birth and length of schooling affect children's attainment at Key stage 1? A question revisited. Paper presented at the British Educational Research Association Annual Conference, York University, 14–17 September 1997.

Silver, H. (1984) Some early childhood projects: history and policy, in C. Adelman, B. Perry, H. Silver, V. Walkerdine and M. Willes, *Early Childhood Education: History, Policy and Practice*. Reading: Bulmershe College of HE Research Publications.

Steedman, C. (1982) *The Tidy House*. London: Virago.

Sylva, K., Roy, C. and Painter, M. (1980) *Childwatching at Playgroup and Nursery School*. London: Grant McIntyre.

Sylva, K., Siraj-Blatchford, I. and Johnson, S. (1992) The impact of the UK National Curriculum on preschool practice. *International Journal of Early Childhood*, Vol. 24, no. 1, pp. 41–51.

Thorne, B. (1993) *Gender Play*. Buckingham: Open University Press.

Tizard, B. (1974) *Early Childhood Education*. Windsor: NFER-SSRC.

Tizard, B. and Hughes, M. (1984) *Young Children Learning*. London: Fontana.

Tobin, D., Wu, D. and Davidson, D. (1989) *Preschool in Three Cultures: Japan, China and the United States*. New Haven, Conn., Yale University Press.

Tough, J. (1976) *Listening to Children Talking*. London: Ward Lock.

Trevarthen, C. (1992) An infant's motives for speaking and thinking in the culture, in A. H. Wold (ed.) *The Dialogical Alternative*. Oxford University Press.

Tyler, S. (1979) *Keele Preschool Assessment Guide*. Windsor: NFER.

Tymms, P. (1997) *Young Children in Reception Classes*. London: SCAA.

Wells, G. (1986) *The Meaning Makers*. New Hampshire: Heinemann.

Wood, D., McMahon, L. and Cranstoun, Y. (1980) *Working with Under Fives*. London: Grant McIntyre.

Index

Printed in the United Kingdom
by Lightning Source UK Ltd.
114292UKS00001B/412-447